Sermon Suggestions in Outline

Sermon Suggestions
in Outline

by

R. E. O. WHITE

LONDON
PICKERING & INGLIS LTD.

PICKERING & INGLIS LTD.
29 LUDGATE HILL, LONDON, E.C.4
26 BOTHWELL STREET, GLASGOW, C.2

SBN 7208 0043 9

Printed in Great Britain by
Lowe & Brydone (Printers) Ltd., London

Preface

Sermons lacking outlines are neither well delivered nor easily remembered: but outlines lacking content and message offer no nourishment to the hearer and little help to the hard-pressed preacher. The following "suggestions" are therefore somewhat fuller than "outline sermons," but development and adaptation are nevertheless left to each man in his local situation. Festivals and special occasions appropriate to each half-year are not overlooked, and outlines for the Lord's Supper, for younger people, and for missionary gatherings, are included.

If these skeletons are used of God to help others explore and expound the everlasting gospel, the author will be deeply grateful.

Contents

1. *Eye Hath Not Seen*

" 'What no eye has seen, nor ear heard, nor the heart of man conceived, what God has prepared for those who love him,' God has revealed to us through the Spirit" — I Corinthians 2:9, 10

Introduction

> *I know not what awaits me*
> *God kindly veils my eyes. . . .*

Moderns fret at this disability: we believe we could decide more wisely, plan more successfully, prepare for eventualities more adequately if we could foresee tomorrow. We question if it is "kindness" that hides the way ahead. Paul holds that *God* has hidden it, and it is better so!

I. The Mystery Profitable

A. Eagerness to know the future arises from the inveterate habit of valuing wisdom, success, knowledge, ease, above all. *Intellectually,* foresight seems invaluable, but for nobility of *character* it is better not to know the future.

B. Anticipation rarely adds greatly to delights: it often brings disappointment — all the greater because we waited so long. It often multiplies troubles and magnifies fears out of perspective: it unfits us to face them. Faith is a bulb that needs darkness to root well. When

> *the steps of faith*
> *Fall on the seeming void and find*
> *The Rock beneath*

then faith finds itself disciplined, deepened, developed, by mystery.

C. The Disciples asked Jesus about the future plans of God. They received the firm reply, so unwelcome to us: "It is not for you to know. . . ." For them, to foresee all would have frightened beyond bearing. Sufficient to each day is its hardships: tomorrow's evil without tomorrow's grace would be unnerving.

So it is providential and profitable that the future remains "a riddle wrapped in a mystery inside an enigma."

II. The Mystery Partial

> *God, stooping, shows sufficient of His light*
> *For us in the dark to rise by,*
> *And we rise. . . .*

9

A. There is light enough to walk by. The Psalmist's life is dark and problematical, but he yet exclaims, "Thy word is a lamp . . . a light . . . to my *path*."

    1. Broad outlines of duty are plain to hearts ready to obey.

    2. Directions of conscience come clearly to those prepared to hear.

    3. Experience is a divine teacher who never shirks her task.

    4. Intuitions of faith are sure for those courageous enough to trust.

B. We know not what awaits us, but we know whom we have believed. When in I Corinthians 13 Paul again reminds us of the mystery of experience — "through a glass darkly — know in part" — he adds "now abideth faith, hope, love." Mystery is only partial: God reveals by His Spirit all we *need* to know.

III. The Mystery Prepared

A. What is mystery to us is clear to God. Israel thought the wilderness way long, roundabout, wearying, and haphazard. It still seems so as we read the list of halting-places. Long afterwards, the Psalmist expressed the wisdom of hindsight: "He led them by a straight way"; "Known unto God all his ways from the beginning"; "He knoweth the way of the righteous"; more wonderful still: "He knoweth the way that *I* take." My times are in his hand, who doeth all things well.

> *Meanwhile, I cannot tell why things are so:*
> *But this, "Thou doest well," I surely know:*
> *The clouds may veil the sun, and tears my eyes —*
> *Still reigns my Lord beyond those curtained skies.*

B. The old promise to Israel entering Canaan, "He it is that goeth before you," is elaborated in words that fit every new experience awaiting God's people: "the land whither ye go is a land of hills and valleys — a land which the Lord thy God careth for: the eyes of the Lord are always upon it, from the beginning of the year even unto the end of the year."

C. Things which are hidden are still things prepared: life is largely a matter of overtaking God's great preparations:

    1. Prepared salvation before the face of all peoples;

    2. Prepared kingdom, from before the foundation of the world;

    3. Prepared table, in the presence of mine enemies;

    4. Prepared place, among the many mansions;

    5. Prepared city, as goal, aim, destiny.

D. Is ours a "see what comes" attitude, a "getting our own way" attitude, or a "catching up with God's preparations" attitude? We step into the unknown — but God has prepared it.

IV. The Mystery Promising

A. Our text is heavy with expected *good* — what else would love prepare? The prophet whom Paul is quoting spoke to Judah's despair; he pleaded for God to come, to rend the mountains, to destroy empires and tyrannies, to break the chains of exile, to bring Judah home. To meet despairing unbelief, he bids: Expect great things — expect the incredible! You never saw, heard, caught rumor or report of the like of it; or imagined in your innermost heart! Yet God will do it.

B. And it happened. Taking up the words, Paul presses the prodigal fullness of God's promises — all confirmed ("yea") in Christ. Complacency impoverishes, but going forward with God to learn, explore, experience, *all* He has prepared — is adventure unending.

Isaiah says that the promise is for those who "wait" for God.

Paul says that it is for those who "love" Him.

2. *Aspiration and Achievement*

"They set forth to go to the land of Canaan. When they had come to the land of Canaan, Abram passed through. . . ." — Genesis 12:5

Introduction

A. Later generations of this family were to discover the great gulf between setting forth and coming to — a forty years' gulf. To set forth means aspiration, desire, ambition, attempting. To come to . . . entails fulfillment, arrival, success, thankful completion. So many set out who never arrive.

B. Abram set out for a new faith, a new home, a new way of life: he felt within him the stirrings of a new age, the inbreaking of a new revelation, the beckoning of new voices to a new adventure. He was a soul setting forth in the dawn of history to seek a new and living faith, to live a new and richer life, to build a new and lovelier home, to obey a new and higher law.

C. Spiritual aspiration always has these elements. There is a glow of new faith in the baptismal hour, the thrill of new married love in vows beside the Lord's table, an ardor of new dedication in the offers of life-service. There is an upreach of faith and dedication as another life sets out for Canaan.

D. But arriving? Terah set out, settled at Haran, halfway, and died there. Many get no farther!

1. Often the *distance* disheartens, till resting-place becomes lodging, dwelling, and grave.

11

2. *Fear* discourages — "The Canaanites dwelt then in the land."
Cowardice defeats ambition as often as does laziness: we lose nerve,
and hope.

3. The *old life* pulls — "Haran" is named after Terah's youngest son,
buried at Ur. Old life, friends, interests, habits so often reclaim
us. We settle for compromise — halfway between old life and new.

E. The enormous leakage from the Church is a real problem. Minis-
ters and keen Christians become frustrated, discouraged, enticed, defeated, lost — "Ye did run well, who hinder?" How can we bridge
the gap between aspiration and achievement? We need:

I. The Conviction That God Commands

"If the Lord command thee . . . then shalt thou be able to endure"
(Exodus 18:23). Presumably Terah agreed with Abram to set out, but
he did not aspire deeply enough to get to Canaan.

A. So often our professed "leadings" are our own hidden motives.
Many talk too glibly, saying "The Lord led me to. . . ." Only a
deep and remaining conviction of *command* — not unstable, emotional,
impulsive — will get us all the way. We have so many unfinished tasks,
incomplete attemptings, unfulfilled enthusiasms!

B. Joshua, taking Moses' place, was assured of God's presence and help,
but God reminded him very firmly, "Have not I *commanded* you. . . ?"
The Hebrew Christians, wavering, uncertain, turning back, are warned
of the *command* in the gospel and of the judgment on disobedience.

C. Inclination, persuasion, and the attraction of rewards prove insufficient for long strain, and there is frequent disappointment. Divine
command lends sinew to character and toughness to conscience. I
must go on when, before God, "I can do no other!"

II. The Foresight That Measures Commitment

A. Jesus warns sharply against ill-considered undertakings, high vows,
far-reaching aspirations, born of emotional situations or shallow, impulsive natures. Offers of discipleship are sifted by deliberately
sharpening costliness (Luke 9:57, 58), immediacy (Luke 9:59, 60), and
irrevocableness (Luke 9:61, 62) of commitment. Some are "not
fit"; some "cannot be" disciples — for want of seriousness of purpose.

B. Discipleship is a tower-building, demanding (Luke 14:28) forethought, estimation, pre-judgment of demands and resources: the
unfinished tower rightly mocks the ambition of the stupid builder.

C. Discipleship is a war, demanding careful calculation of risks, costs,
forces, consequences (Luke 14:31). Rash undertaking, inviting inevitable
defeat, brands the challenger a fool. A cool, common-sense measure-
ment of what we are setting out upon is necessary to carry aspiration
forward to achievement.

D. If this seems to make religious commitment cold, heartless, un-emotional, note that warmth of feeling without clearly defined and per-sistent purpose is *not* conversion or consecration. The great saints were ever shrewd, deliberate souls; W. R. Inge, an acknowledged scholar in the history of Christian mysticism, declares:

> All the great mystics have been energetic and influential, and their business capacity is specially noted in a curiously large number of cases. Plotinus was often in request as guardian and trustee; St. Bernard showed great gifts as an organiser; St. Teresa, as an ad-ministrator; St. Juan of the Cross displayed the same qualities. John Smith was an excellent bursar of his college, Fénelon ruled his diocese extremely well, and Madam Guyon surprised by her great aptitude for affairs. Henry More was offered posts of high responsi-bility.

G. K. Chesterton speaks, in connection with St. Francis of Assisi, of "that curious and almost stunning shrewdness which the unworldly can sometimes wield like a club of stone." Christian commitment is not less heartfelt for being deliberate: T. R. Glover well described the highest kind of piety as "the thought-out life."

III. The Patience that Sustains Consistency

A. Even strong convictions of God's will, and clear considered commit-ment to it, may fail of achievement without "the patience of the saints." The race is not to the swift but to those who "run with patience." We count them happy who endure: he that endureth (said Jesus) shall be saved.

B. Good intentions necessitate long persistence; sincerity is not enough, nor is prayer, without continuance. Spiritual towers are built brick by brick; spiritual wars won battle by battle; spiritual harvests gained seed by seed; great lives lived day by day.

> *We cannot kindle when we will*
> *The fire that in the heart resides,*
> *The spirit gloweth and is still,*
> *In mystery our soul abides:*
> *But tasks in hours of insight will'd*
> *Can be through hours of gloom fulfill'd.*

Thus patience harvests slowly the gains of the great hours and the deep experiences. The road from Ur to Canaan, from aspiration to achievement, is paved with persistence and trod with patience — or we never arrive.

3. *The Perpetual Promise*

"He has said, 'I will never fail you nor forsake you'" — Hebrews 13:5

Introduction

Great virtue and significance are in that "He has said": for the words quoted occur in Genesis 28, Deuteronomy 31, Joshua 1, and I Chronicles 28, and are clearly echoed in Psalm 37. Plainly the promise is eloquent, both of God's consistency and of man's unchanging experience through all generations. It is a refrain in the testimony of the saints, one of the many promises that "find their Yes" in Christ (II Corinthians 1:20). God "loves to be fair" (Psalm 37:28), hence there is something timeless and unchanging about His dealings with His people.

The perpetual promise is repeated:

I. To Varying Types of People

God's constancy is illustrated by their varying characters:

A. To Jacob, running from home, brother, father, sin and God: he received a wonderful fivefold promise (Genesis 28:15). There was no correspondence between God's undertaking and Jacob's deserving — all was of grace.

B. To Israel, in the final address of aged Moses after forty wasted years of wandering, murmuring, folly, faithlessness, disobedience (Deuteronomy 31:6). Again, pure grace.

C. To Joshua, promising, but as yet untried, apparently timid and uncertain (Deuteronomy 31:7-8 and Joshua 1). Grace makes the promise at the outset, before the trial.

D. To Solomon, also untested — having potential of great wisdom and good, of great evil and folly. Yet David speaks of the divine undertaking reinforced with personal testimony — "*My* God" (I Chronicles 28:20).

E. To the Psalmist, who clearly echoes traditional words — again adding testimony, especially to the unfailing divine provision of needs (Psalm 37:25-28).

F. To the Hebrew Christians, tempted to "let slip," "draw back," "cast away confidence." Again there is special reference to needs supplied (Hebrews 13:5).

This list includes many very different people: none yet proved deserving — but divine faithfulness rests on God's unchanging grace.

14

The first and last thing to say about this promise is that "it rests on God."

II. On the Brink of Great Things

A. All stand on the threshold of great enterprise for God:

1. Jacob, to recover from bad failure, to fulfill destiny already endangered by want of character.

2. Israel, to enter and possess, unitedly, the promised land, and hold it for God, there establishing a nation to witness for God.

3. Joshua, to lead, rule, discipline, encourage Israel, to overcome foes, consolidate possession and establish the new community.

4. Solomon, to build the Temple, creating focus for Israel's faith, worship, witness, and communal life.

5. The Psalmist appeals for deeper trust, truer assessment of righteousness and wickedness, and quiet obedience — the enterprise of committing life wholly to God.

6. The Hebrews, to hold on in severely testing circumstances, increasing poverty through loss of inheritance, repeated fines, constant peril through persecution, threats. These believers are challenged to live in need without covetousness, in danger without cowardice.

B. To those who attempt, or suffer, for God, the promise holds: not for lazy, unconcerned, uninvolved. "God grant me work while my life shall last, and life till my work is done" — and unforsaking faithfulness till tasks undertaken are accomplished.

III. On Condition of Faithfulness

A. Though previous merit is not demanded, the promise has one condition. Jacob is to see out the fulfilment of divine purpose; Israel to be strong and fear not; Joshua to be strong and very courageous; Solomon to be strong and courageous to build; the Psalmist appeals for great faith; the letter to Hebrews is full of serious warning, earnest appeal to hold fast, to be followers of them who through *faith* and *patience* inherit the promises.

B. Promise does not depend upon deserving: but we make fulfillment impossible if *we* forsake God, and fail Him. Given our willingness, despite all fears and failures, to go on with God, He will *never* fail, never forsake.

*are you He who is to come
or should we seek for
another?*

4. Seeking God

"Seek the Lord while he may be found,
    call upon him while he is near;
let the wicked forsake his way,
    and the unrighteous man his thoughts;
let him return unto the Lord . . ." — Isaiah 55:6, 7

Introduction

A. The great prophet of the Exile, striving to rouse a defeatist, materialist nation to better life and enduring satisfaction, cries, "Seek the Lord."

B. In the day of social and moral decay, Amos insistently cried "Seek the Lord" (Amos 5).

C. An individual heart beset by suffering, personal tragedy, near-despair cried "Oh that I knew where I might find Him" (Job 23:3).

D. Eleven disciples, facing collapse of hopes, perplexing rejection of Christ, fear of defeat, implored "Show us the Father" (John 14:8).

E. Search for God is the perpetual cry of: the philosopher seeking the meaning of existence, the moralist seeking dynamic for reform, the sorrowing seeking consolation and hope, the saint seeking a vision of eternal beauty, common hearts seeking lost innocence and happiness. The Bible's answer to this deep and universal hunger is twofold:

I. The Avenues of Search

Jesus directed seeking —

A. *Look around you.* Your Father feeds birds, clothes flowers, sends rain on just and unjust, knows your need, causes the sun to rise, speaks through seed, trees, corn, seasons. Nature is the living garment of God — the Father's world. Find Him by His hallmark on His handiwork.

B. *Look behind you.* "Search the Scriptures"; "Have you not read . . . ?"; "It is written"; "You know the commandments." The Old Testament record of experience and revelation is a source-book, text-book, delight, and armory for Christ. "History God's patient explanation to man of eternal principles" — and behind history the self-revealing Lord of History. Find Him by His footprints on the sands of time.

16

C. *Look within you.* "What think ye . . . ?" "Which of you that is father . . . ?" "How say ye . . . ?" "Why judge ye not even of yourselves . . . ?" "Which of you that has a friend . . . ?" The appeal is to the best intuitions of the souls God has made — *not* to "the divine in man," but rather to man as bearing still his Maker's image. This is clear in "If ye then *being evil,* know how to give good gifts . . . how much more your heavenly Father. . . ." Find Him by His fingerprints upon our own nature.

D. *Look at Christ.* "He that hath seen me hath seen the Father"; "No man knoweth the Father save the Son and he to whom the Son will reveal Him"; "No man cometh unto the Father but by Me"; "All power is given unto Me — the Father hath committed all judgement unto the Son"; "We beheld His glory . . . as of the only begotten of the Father . . . no man hath seen God, the only begotten . . . hath declared Him." Find Him by His self-revelation in the person, words, character, life, death, resurrection, and saving power of Christ.

These avenues of discovery are not inaccessible to any — why then do so few find Him in radiant, intoxicating, victorious living? If God is trying to get through, why are so few receiving Him loud and clear?

Because such a search *must* have spiritual, inescapable conditions.

II. The Conditions of Discovery

A. *Be still and know that I am God* — the condition of *quietness.* Some of the greatest things in life are said in whispers — mother to babe, lover to sweetheart, at death, in private prayer: God never shouts anyone down. Consider Elijah on Horeb — God spoke not in an earthquake, a wind, a fire, but in a "voice of a great stillness." Even in sanctuary we are not quiet enough to hear God; we talk too much to listen. The world is too much with us — we too much with ourselves. We must learn quiet mind, heart, and tongue — look on life with quiet eyes, copy Jesus in search of solitude. Not time, but quietness, is the rarest modern opportunity.

It is a matter partly of arrangement of life: partly of self-discipline, partly of practice. Otherwise we shall not find God. "When He comes upon the soul He hath no quiet landing-place."

B. *He that willeth to do shall know* . . . — the condition of *willingness.* We cannot expect our experience of God to leave us unchanged — in direction, values, perspective, or character. Because revelation is addressed to the whole personality, acceptance implies realignment of the whole life: obedience is the 'organ' of discovery; willingness to be changed by the truth, the God we encounter, is a prerequisite of certainty. The pure in heart (sincere, unmixed in motive) see God. Sincerity is indispensable to spiritual insight. To be willing to do as God enables and commands is the path to understanding. Resistance and rebellion never discover God.

C. *He that cometh to God must believe . . . He is rewarder of them that diligently seek Him* — the condition of *confidence*. The crux for most is belief, faith, in the *possibility* of finding God. "If with all your hearts. . . ." "He that seeketh findeth."

The real ground of this confidence is not our informed, sincere seeking of God, but His search for us. He is the seeking Shepherd, the searching Housewife, the watching Father (Luke 15). "The Father seeketh such . . ."; "the Son of Man came to seek . . . that which was lost." God is more than willing to be found — He sets out to meet us, and stirs us to seek Him.

D. *"Let wicked forsake his way . . . unrighteous his thoughts, and let him return . . ."* — the condition of *penitence*.

"God resisteth the proud"; "Rend your hearts . . ."; The Pharisee and the Publican were both "religious" men, but the latter alone found God. The Pharisee "prayed with *himself."*

"Avenues of Search" are open to hearts prepared for quietness, willingness, confidence, penitence.

And Christ will conduct you home.

5. *None to Himself*

"None of us lives to himself, and none of us dies to himself" — Romans 14:7

Introduction

A. The poets argue: one declares "no man is an island"; another, that "in the sea of life enisled . . . we mortal millions live alone." The truth lies underneath both statements: islands do not float! get deep enough, you find them joined together. The social nature of man is no discovery of twentieth-century psychologists: Christianity insisted from the beginning that mere individualism is a distortion of natural order — a half-truth. None lives entirely in a private world, completely on his own resources; we enter life as we leave it, helpless and dependent; liking it or hating it, admitting or pretending otherwise, we are bound with our neighbors in the bundle of life.

B. Admittedly, this is also a half-truth: society exists only in individuals; they are concrete realities, whereas "society" is an abstraction. "The masses" are you, him, her, the others. Hence the *quality* of every group depends on its constituent units; individual conviction and conscience remain the source of social good.

C. The importance of the individual must not eclipse our inter-relatedness. Souls have roots, stretching into other souls; minds have aerials, catching messages constantly from other minds; life is liquid and personality is porous — none *lives* in insulation from his fellows.

18

I. The Triple Cord of Inter-relation

Paul discussed vexatious questions of conscience (how to observe holy days, meats offered to idols, intoxicants) bound to divide a Church mixed in culture, race, and experience. Each must decide for himself, neither despising nor judging his brother; each persuaded in his own mind, as giving account to God. That establishes freedom of conscience, but freedom must be exercised responsibly: we cannot decide *only* for ourselves — we are inextricably bound together.

A. *Conversion binds us together.* We are part of a kingdom, set within the Church, members of the Body, one in a family of brethren. New birth, no less than natural birth, is into a community; conscience is no longer a private concern. The sin from which we turned was essentially self-centered, and we cannot return to that. As brother to all for whom Christ died, you cannot pretend to be God's only child!

B. *Inheritance binds us together.* *Physically*: itemise the average breakfast table — we inherit the earth each morning! *Mentally*: beneath the conscious borrowings through speech, books, life, there lies a still deeper spider's-web of mental inheritance. *Spiritually,* a corporate experience is conveyed through events we never witnessed, in scriptures we never wrote, through a Church we found here when we came, enshrined in lives that have touched ours savingly. Mere individualism here is a mirage, an ungrateful pretense.

C. *Devotion binds us together.* We cannot escape Him by running away into some private world: we are the Lord's — bound in the bundle of life with Him. He chose to be involved in how we live and die: He united us with Himself and nothing shall separate us. Thus our decisions and actions are of concern to Him, and He is not *our* Lord *only* — all men must give account to Him. The bonds that bind us to our brethren run through His hands — and His heart.

II. The Triple Consequences of Inter-relation

In this inextricable relationship lies the deepest truth about the Church: but it has also direct practical consequences:

A. *No man sins to himself.* Every secret disloyalty, every hidden vice, affects the person you are, and so through our social unity contributes to, or corrupts, others. Press, radio, gossip ensure that no private scandal remains private, but whether publicity magnifies or not, a man's inner life casts shine or shadow on all near him. Influence on others is immeasurable; responsibility for others inescapable. To make another "stumble" is to share his guilt.

B. *No man suffices for himself.* When we *forget* our roots in a place or community, cut loose (e.g., in retirement) and begin somewhere else, we find ourselves homesick for where we belong. Sometimes the roots *wither.* The effort of friendship, the humility to seek reconciliation, the patience to understand — these may prove too much trouble and we let the links break, grow within ourselves, lonely, alienated, antagonistic, blaming others, not ourselves, for the shrivelling of our souls. Whenever we try to live to ourselves, something must die.

C. *No man signifies for himself.* Our inter-relatedness means that we matter to others, they to us: even the loneliest, by thus entering and affecting other lives, become important. The deep belief that shadows many, that they live unnoticed and die unmissed, is just not true. Moreover, through inter-relatedness God uses us for each other: we co-operate with or oppose Him in widening circles. We live, and shall die, in the sight of the Lord — important to Him.

6. *Bifocal Faith*

"Cast all your anxieties on him, for he cares about you" — I Peter 5:7
"If any man would come after me, let him deny himself and take up his cross and follow me" — Matthew 16:24

I. High on a Chinese hillside, in the foothills near Hong Kong, stands a Christian settlement, a "retreat." In its heart is a tiny chapel. A traveler entered through a low door, faced at once a clear window looking across a low valley, a green plain, toward the opposite hillside, terraced with bright barley crowned with wild azaleas, beneath a deep clear sky. The view was glorious, but as he knelt, alone, he caught sight of a plain white cross above the window. Above this cross was the Chinese version of the text — "Lay down thy burden."

A. This man had come many miles with a heavy heart. He had seen much of trouble, poverty, disappointment — invading armies, then an invading ideology, countering Christian witness and work. The whole wearisome business of taking the Christian way of life to lethargic resistant people oppressed him — costly past, unrewarding present, enigmatic future. Here was the answer — "Lay down thy burden" — upon God: at the cross where Jesus took all burdens upon Himself.

B. The man gave himself to meditation: *the Lord hath laid on Him — Behold the Lamb that beareth away the sin of the World — Come unto me all ye that labor — Cast thy burden upon the Lord.* Meditation turned to prayer: he rose refreshed, knowing that the burden was not his alone, but Christ's, God's. He could go on serving, for God was carrying the *future,* the *work,* and the *worker.* He had laid down his burden at God's feet.

II. Turning, he bowed to pass through the low door, and he saw, placed where he could not miss it, "Take up thy cross." Suddenly he knew he could not leave the burden of the world with God alone, for he was called to *share* the passion of Christ, to enter redemptively into the world's need, to take Christ's yoke upon himself, to take his *own* cross for salvation of China. This also was the Gospel truth!

20

Passing into sunshine, he felt soothed and stimulated; lighter of heart, yet more intent of purpose; poised between two poles of Christian experience, seeing through the double lens of Christian faith:

1. *Lay down your own burden* of weariness, sin, trouble, regret, self-pity, despondency;

2. *Take up His Cross* of duty, commission, work, prayer, compassion, concern, consecration.

III. This twofold implication of Christian message is inescapable:

1. *The Invitation of Christ* to sinful, weary, fearful, lost men, to find release, salvation, comfort, ease, peace;

2. *The Challenge of Christ* to lazy, selfish, indifferent, indisciplined men, to follow Him in danger, pain, toil, strenuous opposition to world's evils and ills; to rest in His work for us, to rise to His work for men.

A. *The dual implication accords with the true nature of faith.*

1. *The faith that takes* — "Nothing in my hand I bring . . . ." "Naked come to Thee for dress, Helpless look to Thee for grace. . . ." "More than all in Thee I find. . . ." This faith comes simply, humbly, confessing utter need, and takes Christ at His word and gift.

2. *The faith that gives* — endlessly, joyously: "Take my life . . . my hands . . . my voice . . . my silver. . . ." "Were the whole realm of Nature mine, that were a present far too small."

The whole motive power of Christianity lies here: the answering *gratitude* that cannot respond enough to redeeming *grace*. "Faith" comprehends both.

B. *The dual implication accords with the true nature of Christian experience,* which embraces both *peace* and *conflict* (John 16:33). *"In Me peace"*: "Ye shall find rest to your souls" — release of tensions, restored harmony and quietness of Soul. The characteristic experience of Christian hearts is forgiveness, acceptance, assurance, the sense of being *loved*.

Yet, *"in the world, conflict"*: tribulation, facing opposition, standing up for Christ, self-denial, sacrifice. The characteristic attitude of Christian minds is rearming, courage, contention for righteousness and truth. Christians are to be soldiers of Christ.

Whole tension of Christian character lies here — peace with God and self, war with evil, world and sin.

C. *The dual implication accords with the true nature of Christian hope,* which *both works* and *waits*.

1. *Which works* as those work who have seen Christ's vision of the world redeemed. The faithful are committed to pray daily and perform diligently that His Kingdom come on earth.

21

> *Some day I mean, when world is mended,*
> *And no one's a slave, and no one's poor,*
> *And all the ceaseless wrangle is over . . .*
> *To slip away and live in clover*
> *Walking and talking, taking a rest,*
> *In the countryside that I love best . . .*

Some day! Till then, to watch, work, and war till the Kingdom comes.

2. *Yet which waits,* perfectly aware that no work or warfare of men, even Christian men, can change the hearts of a world which crucified Christ. Christian hope awaits His coming, appearing, Kingdom. His intervention from above, His transformation from within, can alone achieve God's goal.

To lay down our burden and take up His cross thus requires faith, experience, hope. Some lay down their burden, but refuse His cross — remaining useless, selfish, unblessed. Some take up His cross, but do not lay down their burden — finding the Christian life strain, obligation, added burden upon conscience. The complete Christian does *both.*

7. *Capsules*

(Faithful Saying 1)

"The saying is sure and worthy of full acceptance, that Christ Jesus came into the world to save sinners" — I Timothy 1:15

Introduction

A. Slogan-making is not confined to politicians or to modern times. One ancient philosophy was packaged into "Know thyself"; a whole ethical ideal concentrated into "Cultivate the middle way." Although inadequate and sometimes misleading, the slogan is a useful teaching device when it summarizes a complex thought and concentrates attention on an important point.

B. It is used in letters to two young pastors. Timothy and Titus, on the brink of the second generation, are charged to teach and organize new people for a new time. Everything in pastorals is "futuristic": the apostolic age is passing away; pastoral priorities are sound doctrine and strong discipline, that the second generation may receive undiluted the inspiration of the first. Points needing special emphasis, to preserve the proportion of truth, are quoted in the form of current Christian proverbs, memorable maxims, labeled as "Faithful (sure) saying." One such indispensable emphasis is written here.

I. The Evangel Stated

A. Into this capsule the essential ingredients of Christianity are compressed — history, incarnation, Christology, salvation, ethics. The basic fact of the good news is plainly stated: Christ Jesus came; the meaningful purpose of the fact is declared: to save sinners; the effectual power of the fact and its meaning is testified to: a faithful saying, worthy to be trusted.

B. A whole estimate of the human situation is implied in the assumption that men are sinners, and so in peril; a whole theology about Jesus is implied in "came," to deal with sin, rescue men, and be *able* to do so. This is the original apostolic preaching; the message enshrined and enacted in Baptism and Supper; the truth that constitutes the Church a redeeming community of the redeemed. If the Church is to have anything to say to man's condition, she must not move away from this controlling affirmation: "progress" becomes declension if this is left behind. The Church's future lies in faithfulness to this faithful saying out of her past. Faith of all ages is founded in *history*.

II. The Evangel Experienced

A. On the *past event* the accent falls: this the great strength of evangelical doctrine — but it brings its own peril: accurate knowledge and sound belief about what happened long ago does not by itself transform the soul. The history must be made contemporary; the general, impersonal slogan must epitomize *my* experience — else the slogan becomes a snare. This best and neatest capsule must be *taken!*

B. "To save sinners — and I am foremost. . . . I received mercy. . . . I formerly blasphemed and persecuted. . . ." Thus the saving event is not left in the air of history but thrust into the present of personal experience: universal metaphors, theological first principles underlying Christian tradition, general statements about "the Christian view," must all be made particular, and *mine*. In this passage:

    1. The testimony is personalised,

    2. The sin itemised,

    3. The gospel-process exemplified in one sample-life, self-confessed as once sinful but now saved.

The *slogan* is focussed on the *soul* — on Paul's story.

C. Here lies the deepest difference between modern evangelicals and those of a few generations ago? The slogans are much the same, intense personal application played down — in hymns, preaching and even in our prayers. Curious that, in an "existential" age, to be "personal" should become serious breach of evangelical good manners!

D. Yet faith cannot be perpetuated by formulae, capsules, alone. When the new generation recites "Christ Jesus came to save sinners," it shows itself well-informed. Only when it adds "Of whom I am foremost . . ." does it reveal itself Christian.

8. *The Profit Motive*

(Faithful Saying 2)

"Train yourself in godliness; for while bodily training is of some value, godliness is of value in every way, as it holds promise for the present life and also for the life to come. The saying is sure and worthy of full acceptance" — I Timothy 4:8, 9

Introduction

Timothy's "oft infirmity," of body and of spirit, finds echo in the preoccupation of the pastoral epistles with "healthy" religion: "sound" (doctrine, discipline) means literally "wholesome," "hygienic." The emphasis recalls the equation of sin and spiritual sickness in the Gospels: only the man of faith is "sound" in mind and heart. These words and their context prescribe simple rules for spiritual health:

I. Rich Nourishment

A. "Nourished on the words of the faith and of the good doctrine. . ." is set in contrast to "godless and silly myths"; elsewhere, to endless working out of genealogies and the endless discussion of so-called "scientific" objections. Interminable debates about queer questions, strange passages of scripture, odd angles of Christian teaching, betray *unhealthy* appetite.

B. Some argue heatedly about odd prophecies, test each other's orthodoxy minutely about future events, but could not begin to summarize intelligently the Bible's teaching on prayer; others pore distractedly over scripture's apparent contradictions, but never even see the grandeur of its glorious affirmations; memory recalls one who would discourse learnedly on the size of throat of Jonah's whale, but never mentioned the seven great priorities of Jesus, or the four indispensables without which none shall see the kingdom. The soul needs *truth* for nourishment, not argument, or curiosities. The first rule of health: feed sensibly.

II. Rewarding Exercise

A. *Train* yourself is more exactly "exercise yourself": even physical exercise has *some* value — the admission is grudging because, to the Hebrew mind, the Greek cult of beauty and strength savored of exhibitionism, sensuality, idolatry. But, without reserve, exercise in godliness is entirely profitable, for this life and the next, for physical health and spiritual, for character and happiness, for individual and society, and for all conditions of life.

B. There is possession of faith, as a sort of spiritual reserve against emergencies: but there is something much more valuable, the practical *exercise* of faith in varying concrete situations, as a power of living. There is a generalized belief in prayer, but there is also a personal grasping daily of prayer's immense opportunities — the *exercise* of prayer. There is an intellectual acceptance of the principle of love and the *exercise* of love in living situations. By exercise, faith grows stronger and steadier, prayer grows bolder, more natural, and love makes its discoveries. Exercise in godliness strengthens the muscles of the soul, keeps us from too great intenseness, introspection, self-absorption. Second rule of health: exercise consistently.

III. Steady Growth

A. "Promise for present and future life" implies the steady accumulation of the personal enrichment, the advancing insight and grace, which godliness bestows. Timothy is to impress upon a new generation of Christians this intrinsic value of the good life, as a storing up of good in the healthy, maturing soul.

B. "Pure gain of godliness" is not the first incentive that would occur to most minds; we more readily agree with other assertions (that God desires godliness, that some have its form but not its power, that it is the surest test of truth) which these letters make. But this also is vital: some get their values the wrong way round and suppose godliness is a means to an end (I Timothy 6:5) — a way of obtaining material blessing (an idea familiar in Judaism); the Christian maxim is "Godliness is profitable in itself" — a sure and faithful saying.

C. That godliness has value is beginning to dawn even upon *secular society*.

1. Godliness offers some clue of wisdom and understanding to an age bewildered about life's meaning.

2. It is the buttress of morality and the social code.

3. It is irreplaceable in the training of the young in responsibility and idealism.

4. Some hearts hunger for its comfort in a bleak and forbidding world.

5. Others long for its protection at home from the solvents of fidelity.

These are genuine lessons of experience, and dearly bought.

D. But *the Master* long ago likened the kingdom of heaven to treasure and pearl, the true riches of the soul; it is Jesus who confronts us with this spiritual profit-motive — the inescapable valuation. What shall it *profit?*

E. Our great difficulty is that precious things become taken for granted. "To this end we *toil* and *suffer*. . ." (v. 10) : None proves the value he sets upon faith and worship, truth and prayer, Church or conscience, until these things are threatened or their demands conflict with his love of himself. Will he then hold to them at all cost? Will he *toil* to preserve them and if necessary *suffer* to hand them on to another generation? It is hard to prize highly what comes to us so easily. Yet the faith has no future unless we hold it dearer than life, more precious than success, happiness, or the world.

Third rule of health: grow in appreciation. If our spiritual life is sickly, it will be because we lack nourishment, or avoid exercise, or do not value godliness highly enough — as worth training for.

9. *The Great Exception*

(Faithful Saying 3)

"The saying is sure:

If we have died with him, we shall also live with him;

if we endure, we shall also reign with him;

if we deny him, he also will deny us;

if we are faithless, he remains faithful —

for he cannot deny himself" — II Timothy 2:11-13

Introduction

A. This third "faithful saying" borrows plainly from a baptismal hymn. The verse pattern is obvious; baptismal themes — dying and living with Christ, confessing or denying Him as Lord, the call to endure — these echo clearly apostolic exposition of baptism throughout the New Testament. Comparison with "modern" baptismal hymns (like Joseph Grigg's *Ashamed of Jesus*) shows how timeless are the needs and the prayers associated with the rite. Especially the call to enter into Christ's conflict, to die with Him, to endure.

B. The context underlines again the over-riding concern of the pastoral letters, handing on the faith to a new generation. The second line of Christians must not expect to receive without effort or risk what the pioneers toiled and suffered to preserve. The soldier must concentrate on one occupation, the wrestler learn the rules and train, the husbandman labor and wait, the apostle endure — to gain the prize of their calling. So must Timothy; so must his converts. There is no cheap way to blessing. Indeed there is a threefold correspondence between behavior and blessing:

I. The Correspondence between Dying with Christ and Living with Him

This is the baptismal gospel: "united with Him in a death like His, we shall certainly be united with Him in a resurrection like His." This is, too, the promise of Jesus; taking up the cross, we find our own souls. This is the message of Easter — life discovered through death. To it Paul testifies — "I am crucified with Christ. . . . Christ liveth in me." This summarizes the whole apostolic experience of bearing about in the body the dying of the Lord Jesus and finding also the life of Jesus manifest through them. Only as we take our place with Christ in death to sin, self, and the world, do we live with Christ in power of endless life. If our experience of that *life* is poor, fitful, it is because our identification with that *death* is partial or perfunctory. The correlation cannot be evaded.

II. The Correspondence Between Endurance and Victory

We reign with Him only in the measure that we suffer with Him. Again words of Jesus are the ultimate authority: He that endureth . . . shall be saved. We are overcomers if we hold fast, says John (Revelation); we are more than conquerors, reign in life, if we walk not after the flesh but after the Spirit. Both our submission, and our sharing of triumph are, in Paul's phrase, "led in the train of His triumph." We are victorious, provided we are trophies! For victory is one of the blessings that cannot be *given*. Triumph without the discipline of conflict would destroy us. So Jesus prayed for Peter — that his faith would not fail, not that he might not be tested; and for us all, that we be kept from evil, but not that we might be taken from the world's temptations. Through much tribulation, only, we enter the kingdom. The condition cannot be escaped.

III. The Correspondence Between our Owning Him and His Confessing Us

A. For the third time Jesus' own words lie behind the thought: If any man confess Me . . . him will I confess. . . . The place given to Peter's confession (at Caesarea) and denial (at Jerusalem) in the New Testament is the best illustration of the importance attached in apostolic Christianity to owning Christ before men. *Here,* to confess Him in baptism and deny Him in life is craven — and forfeits His acknowledgment of us. If we are not ashamed to own our Lord, He is not ashamed to call us brethren. In days of persecution, this open, public confession cost much more. Did the remaining few of the first generation doubt whether the oncoming second generation had the courage in them to outface the world? We know they had!

B. The ancient hymn is true: we can expect no more of spiritual vitality, of moral victory, of divine acknowledgment, than our behavior justifies. Then, the great exception:

IV. There Is No Correspondence Between His Faithfulness and Ours

He changes not: our changing moods, failing strength, and faltering vows make no difference to His purpose of grace and patience, His determination to save. He has promised, and cannot forswear Himself. Four times the New Testament emphasizes this: "Faithful is He who called you; who will not suffer you to be tempted above your ability to stand; by whom you were called; who promised." Enjoyment of the Christian life depends on us: endurance of the Christian way depends on Him — given faith and sincerity, we cannot fail. For He will not.

As the gospel is handed down to another generation, this again must be emphasized as an important element of the gospel's full circle of truth: blessing depends on how we behave; perseverance, on the faithfulness of Christ.

10. *Organization Men*

(Faithful Saying 4)

"The saying is sure: If anyone aspires to the office of bishop, he desires a noble task" — I Timothy 3:1

Introduction

A. Versions and editors have great fun arguing whether this can be one of the "faithful sayings" in which important elements of the faith are to be handed down to another generation. The facts are clear: almost all Greek and Latin manuscripts of the New Testament render the words a "faithful, sure saying" — it is quite obviously a quotation, possibly from some familiar prayer for Church leaders, or some early formula of ordination. The doubt of a very few ancient scribes, and more modern scholars, is understandable: the text scarcely sounds like a significant spiritual slogan!

B. Two considerations put it into perspective: *Bishop* means elder, overseer, leader — several in one local congregation (Philippi, Ephesus, e.g.): in no sense a public figure, ruler, or paid official. The saying· implies no yearning for gaiters! The elder's task is honorary, arduous, responsible, testing. The *Bishop,* too, was in the eyes of the authorities the ringleader of the proscribed sect — in times of persecution, the target for accusation; convenor and chairman (possibly) of the forbidden meetings. No position for the ambitious or cowardly!

C. But important: success in handing on the faith would depend on finding right leaders, men of zeal, integrity, understanding, dedication, courage, to organize Church life and perpetuate the vision and experience of first generation. Timothy must hold before his congregation a high conception of their corporate life and loyalties, and of the honor of being a leader within it.

I. The Spiritual Value of Organization

Of course, to some "organized religion" is a contradiction in terms: religion, like love or art, is among least organizable of experiences. As better, more centralized, organization enters Church doors, piety often flies out through the ventilators! But it is not so simple as that:

A. Anything intended to be shared, corporate, must be planned — e.g., worship, prayer, activity together imply that someone must make known a time, place, invitation, order. *Corporateness implies organization* — else there will be chaos.

B. Jesus certainly intended that we remember Him in the Supper, which implies Table, Bread, Wine, a pattern of communal action. Certainly Jesus meant the Church to live and work in loyalty and love — and therefore appointed teachers and leaders. *Obedience implies organization* — or do we know better than He?

C. The apostolic community faced Rome, not as an incoherent rabble of individualists but as close-knit fellowship with one faith, brotherhood, hope, baptism, loyalty, and Name. All one in Christ Jesus. *Apostolicity implies organization* — and not, as some seem to think, divisiveness masquerading as inspiration!

D. Nothing is so spiritual, personal, precious, that it can survive without embodiment and form. Knowledge and culture survive in society only through schools, universities, books; art and music through galleries, halls, orchestras, societies; marriage itself needs the home and domestic circle, however humble; justice and law survive only through courts, classrooms, libraries. Nor can religion survive without grouping, fellowship, joint action, joint prayer — at any rate, not the religion of Jesus. *Common sense implies organization* — or the Church will perish.

E. Those who affect to despise organization are usually themselves unorganizable, unsocial types: often they go out of existing groups and assemblies, decrying organization, to found their own circles, themselves organizing others! We all need the discipline and grace of mutual loyalty to mature and refine character. *Development of character implies organization* — the alternative is perpetual, childish, self-assertion.

In all our preoccupation with abstract principles of truth, and with ecumenicity, we must remember *the intrinsic importance of the local, organized, unified congregation of* believers — having spiritual value and function in its own right; and we must *never* belittle it.

II. The Spiritual Dignity of Leadership

A. Nor should we belittle its leaders. "To aspire to office is to desire a noble task." In the commendation of Epaphroditus to Philippi, of Timothy to Corinth, of the elders of Ephesus, and in the repeated exhortation to the Hebrew Christians to be loyal and *obedient* to those set over them, *no professional status* is implied, but rather — infinitely better — a high spiritual valuation of leadership in safeguarding truth, governing the Church, handing on the faith. The Church is never healthy when all clamor for authority, when office falls into disrepute, when the ministry comes into rivalry with better-paid careers.

B. Such high valuation of Christian office implies — in these letters:
1. acceptance of an exacting ideal of character,
2. keenness to serve,
3. willingness to train,
4. readiness to set an example in suffering as well as in conduct.

One can always tell how a man relates to the cause of Christ by his readiness to be called to responsibility and work, by his diligence in it, or by the ease with which he lays it down.

C. Sometimes leaders seek too great power, need humbling; sometimes those led are lazy, uncritical, acquiescent, need stiffening and stirring to accept responsibility; some, determined to be neither leaders nor led, need converting — to spiritual usefulness and service. Some of our young men and women accept too readily the prevailing denigration of a career in ministerial or missionary work, and ought to look again at home ministry and foreign mission-field before giving their lives to some other calling. To seek leadership is to seek a *good* thing.

D. See behind local organization the universal, timeless cause and the divine Spirit Who is more than place or people, however dear. See behind title and office the opportunity to serve in definite, demanding, concrete ways the Lord we say we love. Far too much so-called service and devotion are self-service and self-willed devotion, unrelated to the corporate purpose of Christ. If in our eyes the local Church is part of His Body and the office offered to us is His call to work, then this faithful saying will no longer sound strange; "If anyone aspires to office he desires a *lovely* task" will cease to seem peculiar.

11. *Essentials*

(Faithful Saying 5)

"When the goodness and loving kindness of God our Saviour appeared, he saved us, not because of deeds done by us in righteousness, but in virtue of his own mercy, by the washing of regeneration and renewal in the Holy Spirit, which he poured out upon us richly through Jesus Christ our Saviour, so that we might be justified by his grace and become heirs in hope of eternal life. The saying is sure" — Titus 3:4-8

Introduction

A. These familiar maxims of a sound and healthy Christianity, scattered through the pastoral letters as guides to young pastors in handing down the faith to a new age, to be underlined in the training of new Churches, are exceedingly practical and pertinent.

1. The foundation of Christian faith lies in history made contemporary in personal experience (I Timothy 1:15).

2. The foundation of blessing lies in behavior, of Christian perseverance in the faithfulness of Christ (II Timothy 2:11-13).

3. The foundation of Christian character lies in the supreme value attached to godliness for its own sake (I Timothy 4:7-9).

4. The foundation of Christian service rests upon a high valuation of the local Church and its leadership (I Timothy 3:1).

5. But the fifth, recalled to Titus, is more vital, and more comprehensive, than any: the foundation of *everything* Christian lies in a gospel experience of the grace of God.

B. Titus is reminded of the gulf between past and present in the lives of his converts, between Christian and pagan ways of life. Yet Christians must remain submissive to rulers, ready to be useful to neighbors; they must avoid all slander and quarreling, be gentle and courteous toward all men. They are far more likely to be arrogant, critical, quick to condemn pagans about them; this they must avoid — after all, it is not very long since they too were foolish, misled, slaves to passion and pleasure, malicious, envious, hated by men and hating one another (vv. 1-3). Thank God they have changed, now, but it is *no credit to themselves.* The soul-shattering experience that came to them in Christ was bound to transform them — but it came entirely of the grace of God. They are people of a gospel character because they are people of a gospel experience: that is to say —

I. **Christians are people to whom something has appeared** — the "philanthropy" of God! The character of God, as goodness and loving-kindness, has been revealed in Christ, breaking into the darkness of pagan superstition and dread like some flaring apocalypse — illuminating life and nature, world and society, men and the future, with unearthly light of goodwill and hope. *God is love* — never again, unfortunately, can the world recapture the blazing novelty of John's assertion, although it still illuminates converts' minds. Yet they did not think it up — it was not their discovery: a divine epiphany broke upon their midnight — it *appeared.* "Then felt I like some watcher of the skies. . . ."

II. **Christians are people to whom something has happened** — they have been saved, washed, reborn, made over. The constituents of conversion are here boldly rehearsed: washing from the past is a cleansing that regenerates; the sow may return to her wallowing in the mire, but the washed converts are different animals! Forgiven, purified, reborn, renewed — how could they live like pagans? A psychological (as well as spiritual) impossibility! Yet the transformation is none of their achieving. *He* saved us — not we ourselves: we are His workmanship.

III. Christians are people to whom something has been given — the Spirit of Christ, "poured out upon us richly. . . ." They therefore draw life from a new source, and face all temptation and adversity with new spiritual reserves: teaching, strength, power, holiness, growth, vitality, joy — all are theirs in the gift of the Spirit. Leaning no longer on environment or heritage for the springs of their mental life, each has a well of personal inspiration and refreshment, independent, sufficient. Of course, then, they live differently from their neighbors. But the new life is not of their creating: the endowment is of God.

IV. Christians are people to whom something has been promised — they are "heirs in hope — hope of eternal life." The wide popularity of the well-named "Mystery Religions" reveals the mood of paganism: peering into gloom surrounding human life, seeking to pierce all veils, especially those of death and the darkness after death. In contrast, to Titus' converts had dawned a sustaining, enriching hope — a future bright with promise. Yet that hope rests not on promise only, but upon experienced fact; already "justified," Christians know themselves heirs: the future will but unfold and complete present experience. They are rich, and will be richer — but it is none of their deserving.

A. Only *graciousness* befits such experience of *grace* (v. 2): courtesy, humility, gratitude must mark their attitude to those still unaware of this glorious gospel. The analysis of evangelical experience is perhaps nowhere more clear or complete than here: Titus is to keep this true and faithful definition before his people, lest they forget how much they have received — and how freely.

B. *Experience* of grace, conveyed through the gospel, is the foundation of character, of sound social relationships, of public service (vv. 1-3); and it is the foundation, no less, of the Church's future. Instruction, education, the communication of ideas are all very well, but ideas must kindle into feeling, instruction introduce to experience. If Christianity is to pass to a new generation, the faith defined and understood must prove itself the vehicle of *life*. Perpetuating Christianity demands not students only but *converts*, not scholars alone but saints.

12. *In the Garden: Beside the Fire*

"Did I not see you in the garden with him?" — John 18:26

Introduction

The challenge of the High Priest's manservant to Peter in the hour of Christ's trial, though sentimental-sounding as a text, is a *real* question, plain, practical, direct, with a serious challenge at the heart of it; it haunts the mind.

Its first requirement — a plain answer.

I. Have you ever been to the Garden?

A. The servant could have asked many of Christ's followers and received a truthful "No."

Thousands had watched miracles, been fed, heard gracious words, reveled in parables, cried "Hosanna," crowded the Temple courts to rejoice in controveries -- thousands who *never* reached the Garden. Only eleven stayed close enough to Christ to reach Gethsemane; eight hesitated in the shadows; three went on under the trees to pray with Jesus — and they fell asleep!

B. Varying levels of spiritual life are illustrated here: some kneel beside the manger who never listen to the teaching; some, who join Jesus on sunny hills, by a peaceful lake, imbibe idealism, contagion of faith, kindly spirit, and wholesome living, leave Him when He sets His face to go to Jerusalem; some follow even to Jerusalem, to the Upper Room, but never into the darkness, confusion, and danger of Gethsemane.

C. Many Christians are shy of going on alone into some Garden of their own to face things out with Jesus and reach surrender: have never wrestled out issues with God, are never forced to their knees to say, about some refused duty or dreaded experience, or personal tragedy, "Thy will be done." For them, religion must always be sweet reasonableness and optimism — not righteous overmuch or holy overmuch or committed too far. Believers need deeper shadows of more intense experience of God — in darkness, discipline, danger, where personal issues clarify, and great souls are forged; where prayer becomes wrestling, obedience costly, and faith narrows to painful surrender — to a career not chosen but imposed, a decision not wished for but demanded, an acceptance reached reluctantly out of struggle, an experience in which the passion of Christ is *shared*.

D. Until this experience is tasted, a whole range of spiritual possibilities remains unexplored, a whole dimension of spiritual strength is never known, the Christian life that has never been in the Garden, kneeling with Christ is shallow, immature, and incomplete.

So first question is: have we been there? Is ours a "Christianity without tears"? a "cheap grace evangelicalism" that accepts all Christ offers, and leaves Him to pray alone in the shadows, refusing our share in the Cross?

II. What, then, are you doing where you are?

This the meaning for Peter — if once in the Garden with Jesus, why now in house of His enemies, warming his hands?

A. The transportation all too familiar. 1. There, in the Garden, the solemn hush, the atmosphere of prayer, the sense of great issues and crucial decisions, the presence of God, the feeling of mystery and the wholesome fear of God, the earnest warning about flesh and spirit and slothfulness: above all, nearer than ever before to Christ, sharing, though imperfectly, His Passion and His Prayer.

2. Here, in the Judgment Hall, noise, ribald laughter, an atmosphere of hostility and scorn, hiding and evasion, abject fear of man. Christ is alone now, and bound. Peter is at distance from Him, and aware of it, yet unable to tear himself away. The disciple "followed afar off"; within sight, sound, and reach of the Jesus he *wants* to love — but not at His side, identified, committed. Warming his hands at the world's fires, he is torn in heart by disloyalty and fear.

There is some such change of scene every time we return to the 'real' world (as we wrongly call it) from Worship, private prayer, Christian fellowship, campaign or festival — back to different place, company, circle, standards, fears.

B. The transformation, also, is all too familiar. 1. In the Upper Room, "Though all forsake . . . Not I"; in the Garden, the flashing sword defending Christ, the deep, sincere regret for slumber. Here, vile oaths, faithless swearing, dread of pain, the craven spirit denying Jesus' friendship and Lordship. We, so often, are different people in different circumstances — out of Church, in a secular atmosphere, away from family, prayerless, drifting from Christ, "afar off," weak, inconsistent, inconstant.

2. The contrast is seen especially, note, in one's *company, conversation* (Thy speech betrayeth) and *cowardice* — refusal to own Christ.

The Garden and the Judgment Hall encompass most Christian lives — and *we* are judged, not Christ.

At our work or entertainment, in our off-guard moments, or during our sullen moods — could such a challenge shake *our* hearts? — Did I not see thee in the Garden — or at the Table — with Him? What, then, are you doing where now you are?

13. *What a Day!*

"Would that even today you knew the things that make for peace!"
— Luke 19:42

Introduction

A. What a day that was! In all three years' astonishing scenes, mounting excitement, none surpasses it for sensation and significance. In the morning, the disciples watched Jesus ride into Jerusalem, heard the echoes stir with the ancient cry — Hosanna! About midday, they had stood with Jesus on the shoulder of a hill overlooking Jerusalem, gazing across the narrow valley to the city. In the evening, they witnessed a public disturbance within the Temple precincts, as Jesus dramatically, vigorously challenged ecclesiastical authorities within their own stronghold, and got away with it.

B. There was enough to talk about far into the night; but it was more likely that each sought bed thoughtful, disturbed, subdued. Each had been:

I. In the Morning, Rebuked by the Divine Lowliness

A. Had seen God's Messiah, riding at last the royal, sacred way into the capital; there were ancient symbols of welcome to any King coming to his coronation, laying down of garments, an avenue of palms, acclamation of people, ancient greeting to the Son of David.

1. Politically-minded men remembered Jehu, a powerful reformer, a king whose revolution overthrew wicked Ahab and re-established righteous reign (similarly greeted, II Kings 9:12-13)

2. Religiously-minded persons recalled Zechariah 9:9, and marveled at the exactness of messianic prophecy. Though the Romans saw nothing significant, the Jews recognized the event as a crucial claim to kingship in God's name.

B. Yet unarmed, He had an escort of peasant-pilgrims, a manner peaceable and mild, a manifesto of "peace," His "charger" a humble donkey. Not so did Israel picture the Messiah; they imagined a flaming figure in the skies, a warrior-Christ taking vengeance on foreign invaders. Not so did the Greeks think of Conquerors, or Romans of Caesars!

Here is: majesty combined with meekness,
authority in garb of deep humility,
power clothed with gentleness,
kingliness content to ride with common folk —
God upon a donkey!

C. So the disciples felt rebuked; they had been arguing, all the way from Galilee, who should be greatest in positions of authority, glory? Here, with the donkey, as later in the Upper Room with a towel, He showed what greatness means — how unassuming, quiet, unpretentious, and meek, *real* power can afford to be. They had things sadly wrong; as they squabbled for pre-eminence, domination, position, "who would give way to whom," God's Messiah-Son rode to His throne on a common donkey, in lowliest guise.

D. Nor have modern Christians yet understood how —

> truth can afford to speak quietly,
>
> authority can afford to wait,
>
> greatness can afford to be ignored.

Real power needs no advertisement-display. Only those *uncertain* of truth, authority or power need to bluster, threaten, protect their dignity!

II. At Midday, Surprised by the Divine Compassion

A. From the brow of Olivet, looking across the valley, the pilgrims first caught sight of Jerusalem. "How beautiful for situation, joy of the whole earth" — white towers, gleaming walls, the great gate of the Temple flashing back the glare of noon, full of ancient glories, had thrilled thousands of pilgrims to the thrice-annual Jewish feasts.

B. As they turned to exclaim to Jesus, they saw His tears falling, His solemn, stricken gaze, and they fell silent to catch the words of His lamentation — "O Jerusalem . . . how oft. . . . If only. . . . But now. . . ." All the beauty of the scene and all the glory of the great past are eclipsed in the horror of the future. The city stands under judgment; rejecting Him, it would be itself rejected. Soon not a stone would be left on stone; the intervening valley would be filled with crosses erected by the Romans for those who erected His. Appalling, self-chosen doom lies ahead!

C. The Galileans were not surprised. The Messiah of judgment had been foretold by the Prophets, John the Baptist, the Apocalyptists. The Messiah's flashing eyes, searing words, scathing condemnation, and vivid portrayals of doom were prophetic stock-in-trade. But Jesus *weeps*: that is incredible!

D. Here is a new, disturbing conception of judgment and of God. Divine judgment is no outburst of "wrath," no tirade of revenge, but a condemnation, a punishment, just, right, inevitable, but foreseen with tears. God's very *justice* is compassionate; His own heart grieves for sinful men. "Like as a Father pitieth children, so Lord pitieth them that fear Him" — and those who do not. This truth is near the heart of the Gospel — suffering of God with men, for sin. "In all their affliction He is afflicted." Wrote William Blake:

Till our grief is past and gone
He doth sit by us and moan.

All ye that pass by, come see if there ever was sorrow like *God's* — for a world He must judge!

Modern Christians do not fully understand this yet. We talk of mercy *or* judgment, not of both. Like the disciples, we are surprised at the compassion of the Judge.

III. In the Evening, Over-awed by the Divine Holiness

Lowly, compassionate Christ is suddenly austere, stern, terrifying, so as to silence all protest, bear down opposition, and challenge authority at the national center, the Temple.

A. It was not simply the buying and selling in the sacred place that stirred Christ to wield the whip, overturn the tables, and drive the traders from the precincts. It was the greed, dishonesty, and avarice, hidden and made acceptable by religion: private gain fattening on public piety by thoroughly despicable means. Only priests could pass animals for sacrifice, so they exercised a lucrative monopoly. Priests demanded Hebrew coinage for Temple dues, and they themselves arranged exchange rates for common Roman coinage. Priests thus arrogated, to their own private profit and their families', the whole area of outer courtyard, which was assigned as the only place where attracted Gentiles could offer worship, for traffic in the requirements of ritual there was wholly under the priests' control!

B. There were frequent popular riots against this cornering of the religious market. Jesus' eyes, voice and searing words ("House of prayer for all nations . . . den of *thieves*"; Mark 11:17) resemble those of a fierce Old Testament prophet, proclaiming righteous demands of holy God upon those who profess worship (e.g., Isaiah 1). God's absolute resistance to everything shady, underhanded, greedy, hypocritical, deceitful, oppressive. All of the Bible insists that ethics and religion belong together: there can be no worship without worthiness, no devotion without moral goodness, no approach to God without clean hands, no seeing God without pure heart. Neither belonging to the priesthood nor operating in sacred precincts will shelter. God is pure and demands a pure people.

Such thoughts filled the last hours of an astonishing day:

1. God *Lowly,* rejoicing in hiding His power, setting aside majesty to ride with humble men;

2. God *Compassionate,* in the midst of judgment suffering with us; in our sin Himself afflicted, crucified.

3. God *Holy,* and demanding holiness in worship.

These are the chief things that belong to our peace, too.

14. *Unblessed at the Cross*

(Good Friday)

"And when they had crucified him, they divided his garments among them by casting lots; then they sat down and kept watch over him there"
—Matthew 27:35

Introduction

A. The ghastly job is done. The excitement of the trial, the frenzy of the crowd, the suspense, and peril of a popular rising, the challenge and counter-challenge between Caiaphas and Pilate, with Jesus tossed between them, is all past. The near-hysterical nationalism that prompted "Crucify Him!" has given place to clever taunts and bitter jeers, and even these die away as others urge "Let be, it is enough!" As the light fades from the sky, tumult is hushed to quiet talking, muffled sobs; they become still and silent, so that they hear what Jesus says to the thief hanging beside Him. In the gathering darkness a sobered crowd, with growing fear and doubt, awaits the end.

B. Soldiers sit and watch, and play at dice. Women stand and watch, a little apart. Some of the disciples — Luke says, later, "all His acquaintance" — wait and watch, fearful for themselves. And "the people stood beholding." The crowd at the foot of the cross has been growing ever since. Probably never in Christian history will so many gather there as on this Good Friday.

C. So Christ planned His Church — disciples assembled around a Table remembering His cross; so Christ foresaw the world-mission of the kingdom — Himself so lifted up as to draw all men unto Him. You and I will be there, as near as time and faith and imagination allow, singing and celebrating, arguing its meaning, proving our orthodoxy with time-honored phrases of interpretation, or perhaps, still somewhat puzzled, a little heart-hungry for the power and blessing we are sure are enshrined in the gospel of the cross — but not yet wholly ours. Some of us will sit among the soldiers — so near, yet unmoved; close to Calvary, but unblessed.

I. The cross of Christ is "emptied of its power" when we grow shy of proclaiming it the only hope of sinful men (I Corinthians 1:17).

A. Festus' taunt, Greek contempt, and the criticism of some Corinthian Christians stung Paul. His disputatious replies to "the folly of wisdom" show sharp feeling. He had eloquence, wisdom, training, and wit to charm and dispute and titivate, but he determined to know nothing but Jesus and him crucified. This self-discipline arose from his conviction that the preaching of the cross was the power of God: to depart from that theme was to forfeit effectiveness; intellectual self-limitation in the content of the message is the price of power.

B. The cross is truly the only hope. Kagawa, from the heart of former Kobe slums, said "Without the cross, the real uplifting of humanity is impossible." Goethe: "I leaned on the little table beside me and hid my tear-stained face in my hands, and who could ever express to me in the dimmest way the experience that came to me then? A secret influence drew my soul to the cross: it was an inward *leaning* — I cannot give it any other name — and in that moment my spirit received a wholly new power of uplifting." Christina Rossetti:

> *None other Lamb, none other Name,*
> *None other hope in heaven or earth or sea,*
> *None other hiding-place from guilt and shame,*
> *None beside Thee!*

C. Therefore, like Paul, we must beware of making the cross of none effect by side-stepping its proclamation. To turn to gimmicks of popular religious appeal, playing down horror and holiness of Calvary as "not what modern people want to hear," to pander to spiritualized hedonism, the always-positive public image, tolerance at all costs, and the preference for being saved by the piety of good music, the cadences of poetic prayer, the wisdom of a cultured spiritual psychology — instead of by the cross of Christ — is to sit with the soldiers, in view of and within reach of the redeeming death of Jesus, unaware of its power. We can gamble our souls away, blind to divine love stretched upon a gallows in order to find a way to forgive a sinful world.

II. Christ will have "died to no purpose" for us if we fail to trust entirely what He did for our salvation.

A. So Paul pleads with Galatians not to shift their ground from faith in free grace of Christ to confidence in themselves, and in their keeping of the Jewish law. Christianity is no do-it-yourself religion. If we could do it ourselves, and if salvation could be ours through piety, almsgiving, contributions to international charity, foreign aid, or understanding Tillich and Bultmann, then Jesus need not have died.

B. Here again Paul speaks with feeling: it was in the matter of *confidence*, in racial descent, learning, family-tradition, and knowledge of the law (Philippians 3), that the Christian shoe most sorely pinched the Rabbi's foot. Boasting, once the immediate personal reward of faithfulness to Judaism, became almost a phobia with Paul; he mentions it, always with strong deprecation, scores of times. In nothing, on no personal issue, did Christianity differ so vitally from Jewish piety than where one placed one's confidence: Jesus spoke unerringly to the heart of the quarrel between Him and Pharisaism, in the parable of

Pharisee and Publican. Paul had to step across the Temple from one position to the other — and it took some doing!

C. It always does. The offense of the cross to Jew and Greek is nothing to its offense to the pietistic mind. It is hard and humiliating to forego reliance on one's own energy, consecration, public service, and private devotion, and to live by faith in the Son of God who loved and gave Himself. But to sit at the cross contemplating our own good works and not His necessary and all-sufficient work, is to sit with the soldiers and see Christ die in vain.

III. We make the cross of none effect and sit unblessed within its shadow, whenever we decline to bear it.

A. Hebrews 6:1f. is a sharp warning against crucifying the Son of God afresh, counting His blood unavailing, and so doing the soldiers' work again: this startling idea arises from the defection of some Hebrew Christians in face of bitter disappointment and perplexity (perhaps at the destruction of Jerusalem, God's city) and at the threat of persecution (12:4; 10:32f.). Many were tempted to turn back, to cast away their confidence in Christ, because it threatened to "pay off" in suffering and loss. To do this is to refuse to share Calvary with Christ, and it implies that by our own choice the cross shall mean nothing for our hearts.

B. The story of David's rejection, in the rebellion of Absalom, reveals several men in varying lights, as some hasten to dissociate themselves from David, and to curse him, to gain favor with the new regime (II Samuel 15:31; 16:1f., 16:5f.); others prove gloriously loyal in David's adversity — especially a foreign levy in David's army, Ittai of Gath (II Samuel 15:19f.), and the aged Barzillai (II Samuel 19:31f., see 17:27f.). Both these men risked all their future on the fate of David, but loyalty held; Ittai's vow (15:21) was: "Wherever my Lord the King shall be, whether for death or for life, there also will your servant be" — a perfect model for ourselves as we are called to go forth with our King in His rejection. Only those who so bear the cross with Christ can know the joy of sharing victory and power. But often the call of Christ clashes with self-will and inclination, and — with innumerable high-sounding explanations, no doubt — we turn to some easier religion. We turn from the cross, as the soldiers turned at last, leaving Him hanging there, making it a tragedy in which *we* have no personal share, in which *we* shall suffer no personal pain. That crucifies Him again.

Illustrations apart, the warning that the very cross of Jesus can stand among us an idle, empty symbol, meaningless, powerless, made of none effect, is solemn indeed. But proclaimed, trusted in, faithfully borne, it is the power of God and the place of salvation.

40

15. *If Christ Has Not Been Raised*

"If Christ has not been raised, then our preaching is in vain and your faith is in vain. . . . If Christ has not been raised, your faith is futile, and you are still in your sins. . . . If in this life we who are in Christ have only hope, we are of all men most to be pitied. . . . If the dead are not raised at all, why are people baptised on their behalf? — Why am I in peril every hour?" — I Corinthians 15:14, 17, 19, 29, 30

Introduction

It is important to remember that Paul writes as a pastor, not as an apologist or a philosopher, or even, primarily, as a theologian. He furnishes arguments, but his concern is always the spiritual and moral soundness of his people, not intellectual debate. So here, even in this great argument about the Resurrection, his chief anxiety is caused by the undermining of Christian confidence and experience by perplexity, doubts, and half-belief. To a church too confused, uncertain, and un-settled by Greek speculation to appreciate fully the Easter message, he sends a solemn reminder that the Resurrection of Christ is not a fit subject for leisurely abstract argument — it is vital to the quality of Christian living. If Christ has not been raised, we have no message for the world, our faith is futile, our hope uncertain, our conflict confused, our baptismal allegiance pointless.

I. If Christ be not raised, we have no message for the world: "our preaching is in vain."

A. This is emphatically true of Paul's own preaching: at Athens (Acts 17:31, 32) the proclamation of the Resurrection was the point at which the sermon was interrupted. Festus explained to Agrippa that Paul asserted Jesus to be alive (Acts 25:19). Paul declared his commission was to witness to this fact (Acts 26:22, 23). Always he declared Jesus to be Lord — "designated Son of God . . . by resurrection" (Romans 1:4) — Christ the hope of glory. Doubtless this emphasis stems from Paul's meeting with risen Christ on the road to Damascus. Resurrection was the crucial point in his own experience of Christ. Perhaps this insight began even earlier, with Stephen's testimony to the risen Christ at God's right hand. Some "Christian" preaching, even some preaching of the cross, would not be "vain" if Christ had not risen: but Paul's would: *Jesus risen* was the basis and spear-point of his proclamation.

41

B. And of ours. The Sermon on Mount, the parables, the Bethlehem idyl, the gracious ministry, sterling character, and inspiring vision — all lose cogency if Christ went out into everlasting darkness. *That* is no message but most profound disillusionment, a horrible warning that *no* effort or love or greatness or inspiration survives or is worthwhile! All turns on *who He is* — the risen, triumphant, everlasting Christ. *This* our message.

II. If Christ be not raised, our faith is futile: "we are yet in our sins."

A. Paul puts it three ways. Our faith is *"in vain"* — empty, as a purse to which we turn in extremity and find nothing, as a water-bottle in the desert which fails us in need, as an idea, a hope, a plan which proves to have "nothing in it." Our faith is *"futile"* — has no point, produces nothing — an idle dream irrelevant to the real world and daily life. For it leaves us as it found us, powerless and without hope. And we are still *"in . . . sins"* — both because it is the Resurrection which demonstrates God's acceptance of atonement (Romans 4:25; 8:33, 34; I Peter 1:21) and because a dead Christ cannot deliver from the power of sin.

B. Easter morning illustrates this. Before daybreak, the Christian band was not careless, hostile, and forsaking, but grieved, wistful, and heartbroken. The group had faith of a sort — memories, great hopes now reluctantly surrendered, great love for the Master, but mixed with fear, perplexity, oppression, feeling of loss, tragedy; they were silent, had nothing to say; there was no sense of deliverance, redemption, or forgiveness through His death. Faith reached out empty hands to a Christ only of memory; minds groped for answers. All their experience of three years seemed vain, futile, and ineffective to deliver — except for wistful longing, sadness, and disappointed hopes.

C. Then He came to them again, and all was changed. The teaching stood, the vision was still there, the memories re-focussed around a living Lord, all was explained (Luke 24:27), and their years with Christ bore fruit in power, deliverance, and joy. Christianity is not a system of ideas plus ideals, vision plus forlorn hope, but companionship with a victorious Lord; *that* faith is purposeful, powerful, and pertinent to our need.

III. If Christ be not raised, our hope remains uncertain: "we are of all men most to be pitied."

A. Because *we* have seen the vision and seen it fade, have loved a glorious Lord and lost Him, have lived in expectation of immortality and found that those asleep have perished, we have lost both worlds, surrendering *this* for the illusory *next*! If Christ be not raised.

B. The deepest shadow on modern Christianity is the dimness of immortality. Heaven has faded, even from our hymns. Destiny is perplexity, not goal. The future is unclear, hope clouded; and with it fades all endurance, persistence, initiative, and worthwhileness of struggle and suffering.

C. This no fitting mood for Christians. He is Risen, "as He said" — keeping His word. R.S.V. clearly renders Paul's point: not just: "if in this life only we have hope" — acknowledging that *already* Christ means much to us, heaven notwithstanding; but: "if we . . . have only hope" (N.E.B. margin: "if it is only an uncertain hope that . . . Christ has given us"). Easter kindles *certainty*, confidence, joy. The world had arguments — "intimations of immortality," the "glorious surmise" before, but Easter brings the risen Christ to set all doubts at rest. Ours is no optimistic intuition, delusive wishful thinking, but argument from experience: "we . . . begotten to living hope by the resurrection of Christ."

IV. If Christ be not raised, our conflict is confused: "why am I in peril every hour?"

"I die every day! What do I gain if, humanly speaking, I fought with beasts at Ephesus? If the dead are not raised, "Let us eat and drink, for tomorrow we die! Do not be deceived. . . ."

A. Paul writes I Corinthians evidently out of great tribulation — "toiling, tears, trials, plot of the Jews, hunger, thirst, ill-clad, buffeted, homeless, labouring, beasts, many adversaries, utterly unbearably crushed, despaired of life itself, received sentence of death. . . ." (Acts 20:19, 34; I Corinthians 4:11-12; 15:32; 16:9; II Corinthians 1:8, 9). The Corinthians too had their troubles; living Christian lives in an utterly pagan seaport city was not easy! Yet all this conflict and struggle was pointless unless they were assured of victory, vindication, by the triumph of Christ.

B. Again the Easter contrast illustrates — the disciples hiding behind locked doors "for fear of the Jews," defensive, backward-looking, striving to conserve what they had seen and felt but with no hope of universal success (so like the modern church). Doors were locked against the enemy, hearts fighting despair, lest strong winds of the Roman world and scornful hatred of the Jews should destroy all Christ had left them. Then He came. And they went out into Jerusalem, forward-looking, attacking, accusing, advancing, marshaled by a Risen Lord, to whom all power had been given, who said "so send I you."

This effect of Resurrection on Christian resistance, attack, and endurance is well summarized in I Corinthians 15:58.

V. If Christ be not raised, our baptismal allegiance is pointless: "if the dead not raised, why are people baptized on their behalf?"

A. This is one of the most obscure verses in the New Testament. There are over thirty possible interpretations. Possibly Paul means it is pointless to swear allegiance in baptism to a dead Christ; more probably he is referring to a heathen (Mystery Religion) custom, and so contends that if *their* baptism implies immortality, how much more ours? Either way, Christian baptism is linked with living Lord and eternal life.

B. We are not baptized to a dead Christ, or to a deader tradition, creed, system of ideals, but to a living Friend who knows, cares, loves, leads, is grieved at our failures, and upholds all who lean upon Him — who will not let us go. It is important to note that the command to baptize disciples is set in the context of the ascension and concluded by Jesus' promise to be with us always (Matthew 28:16-20). As we are planted in the likeness of His *death*, in baptism, so also we are planted in the likeness of His Resurrection (Romans 6:5). Baptism is death with a view to risen, victorious *life* — a loyalty charged with the power of endless life.

C. Bishop Azariah (1874-1945) of Dornakal, first and greatest native Indian bishop, when asked "If you were in village which never heard of Christ, what would you preach about?" answered without hesitation, "the Resurrection." This was the secret of his life, and it is the secret of Christianity, the *message* proclaiming Christ triumphant, *faith* centered in the living Savior, a *call* to conflict marshaled by the victorious Lord, *undying* hope grounded upon radiant certainty, *limitless loyalty* nourished by personal Love.

For now is Christ risen!

16. *After-Easter Insights*

"And behold, there was a great earthquake" —Matthew 28:2

Introduction

A. There was mental and moral upheaval in the minds and hearts of the Eleven and of the whole apostolic company. Vivid contrasts mark the Easter story, contrasts of mood, fear, belief struggling with bewilderment, astonishment; "fools, slow of heart to believe" and also men and women overjoyed, bursting with news; persons slow-footed and sad, yet later swift and tireless, running to tell; some sceptical, others intoxicated with excitement. All these are signs of a psychological and spiritual experience shattering as an earthquake, awesome as an eclipse, demanding radical re-adjustment.

B. All was different, all normal assumptions challenged, everything transfigured with resurrection light.

I. The Resurrection left a clear mark on their thinking about God: henceforth, God of the impossible.

A. Thirty times in the New Testament (11 in Acts alone), God is spoken of as having raised Jesus from the dead ("the God who raised Him from the dead"; or [Christ] "raised by God's own power, by glory of the Father"; "God . . . *able* to raise. . .". Peter and Paul say, "We trust (believe) in God who raised the dead"; "faith in the operation of God who raised the dead"; "believe in our hearts God raised Him from the dead"; "Why incredible God should raise the dead?" Both Romans (4:17, 19) and Hebrews (11:19) define the typical, exemplary faith of Abram as "faith in God who raised the dead" (i.e., living Isaac born from parents "as good as dead"). (See e.g., Acts 2:24, 32, etc.; Romans 10:9; I Corinthians 6:14; II Corinthians 1:9; 4:14; Ephesians 1:19-2:6; Colossians 2:12; I Peter 1:21). Clearly, God is no longer conceived only as Creator, King, Judge, Lord of History and conscience (as in the Old Testament) but now also as the God of Easter, of the impossible, unforeseeable triumph, "who only hath immortality."

B. And this new conception of God was applied to the salvation experience (Ephesians 1:19 - 2:6), apostolic calling (Galatians 1:1), deliverance from danger, distress, and defeat (II Corinthians 1:9). The God of the impossible does wonders for *sinners, servants,* and *supplicants.*

II. The Resurrection totally changed their thinking about the cross.

There were obvious differences in the whole aspect of Calvary. *Before Easter* all was tragedy; *after* Easter, triumph. *Before,* darkness, mystery; *after,* glory. *Before,* all was at an end; *after,* all was at a stupendous beginning. Easter day transfigures Good Friday.

But deeper:

A. The cross had seemed an evil that wicked men, with cruel hands, had engineered (Acts 2:23, 36); it is now seen as accomplished "according to the definite plan and foreknowledge of God" (23): therein "God commended His love toward us" — "it pleased the Lord to bruise Him. . . ."

B. The cross had seemed something that ought not to happen: "This shall never be to Thee. . ."; "Far be it from Thee. . ." — the disciples' indignant protests. Now: "as it is written . . . ought not the Christ to suffer these things. . . ? Christ died according to the scriptures."

C. The cross had seemed the triumph of evil — "This is your hour, and the power of darkness" (Luke 22:53). So the Emmaus walkers also felt (Luke 24:19-21). Now it is seen as the conquest of evil — "He disarmed principalities and powers . . . triumphing over them" (Colossians 2:15). Over death and sin He gives us "victory" (I Corinthians 15:57), and sin shall no longer have dominion over us (Romans 6:14). One eloquent illustration of this change: the disciples come to use the horrible language of crucifixion easily, unconscious of its horror — "I am crucified with Christ . . . buried with Christ . . . crucified-together with Him . . . bearing in our bodies the dying of the Lord Jesus. . . ." The cross was transfigured in *imagination, memory,* and *meaning* — by Easter.

45

III. The Resurrection confirmed and completed their thinking about Jesus.

A. There are hints of something strangely different about Jesus: "appeared in another form" (Mark 16:12) ; "their eyes were kept from recognizing Him" (Luke 24:16) ; "a frightening spirit" (Luke 24:37) — Mary supposes him the gardener; Cleopas thinks He is "a stranger"; the disciples (apparently) mistake Him for a merchant (John 21:4). To the end "some doubted" (Matthew 28:17). "This same Jesus" was not quite the same.

B. There are hints also of changed relationship: "Do not hold Me. . ."; "not yet ascended to the Father. . ."; "to my Father and your Father, to my God and your God." Strange air of withdrawal and distinction: a new level, phase, of relationship. "Though we once regarded Christ from a human point of view, we regard Him thus no longer" (II Corinthians 5:16). The Carpenter, Teacher, Healer, Prophet, the Jesus of sermon and parables, doing deeds of kindness, with children round Him, is seen in Easter light as the Christ of all ages, all men, all races. He is the "diadem of beauty" (Tertullian), "the treasure house of wisdom and knowledge" (Paul), "the King of kings and Lord of lords" (John), "My Lord and my God" (Thomas). The Gospel of the Great Galilean, with high-toned ethic and heroic example, is exposed by the Resurrection as shallow, insufficient. The risen Christ is the universal, timeless, divine Redeemer — no less:

> *The night was dark, the shadows fell*
> *Far as the eye could see:*
> *I gave my hand to the human Christ,*
> *And He walked in the dark with me.*

> *Out of the darkness we came at length,*
> *Our feet on the dawn-warmed sod,*
> *And I knew by the light in His wondrous eyes*
> *That I walked with the Son of God.*

IV. The Resurrection transformed their thinking about the world at large.

A. Like everyone else, the disciples lived under tyranny of material things; the evidence of their senses — things seen, touched, handled — they assumed as ultimately "real." The visible, the concrete, the tangible they reckoned as permanent. Mountains, rocks, firm earth, natural law, physical body were "solid certainties"; but spirit, moral law, heaven, hell were less certain.

B. Yet, at Easter, mountain and earth shaken, solid rock-tomb opened, shut doors passed, dead Christ alive before them — all the material world melts and Spirit stands forth changeless, timeless, real; and personal relationships, truth, and love are permanent, immortal. Suddenly, the future is bright, all doors are open, the world is after all a spiritual home, and man is the child of the eternal. Paul draws the brave conclusion: "We look not at things seen . . . temporal: things not seen are eternal."

Refracted in the after-glow of Easter:

1. God was different;
2. The cross was different;
3. Christ was different;
4. The whole world was different
— a great earthquake indeed!

17. *Danger — Men at Worship*

"Such the Father seeks to worship him" — John 4:23

A cluster of portraits showing men at their most sacred moments; documentary film-strip on the practical relevance of worship:

A. One of the world's greatest was learned in all wisdom of Egyptian civilization. Born leader of men, lawgiver, statesman, he created a nation out of slaves, helped to shape a religion out of a sparse tradition of faith. Strong and saintly, he was one of history's giants.

Yet see him at moment of failure — alone, keeping sheep, great gifts wasted, hiding, afraid. He has attempted to sympathize with his people — Israel — in their subjection to Egypt, has intervened in quarrels, killed an Egyptian, and fled. His first well-meant intention to deliver his people from bondage has ruined all his chances, so he is shepherding, alone, in the desert of Midian. He finds a bush aglow — curious, draws near, hears a voice, meets God; "Take off shoes. . . ." The hour of worship is the turning-point of his life. His long objection and fears are brushed aside, and he is sent back to Pharoah to try again. He learns *in worship* (a) that no failure is final, if we have God; (b) that God's purpose holds, whatever our feeling or frustration. God's purpose, not ours, is supreme.

Worship can *redirect* life into new channels.

B. A young man, on the threshold of a tremendous task, both military and political, inheriting an unfinished enterprise with little left of the vision and drive of the pioneers. An ill-equipped, disunited, untrained agglomeration of tribes, weary of migration, is to be welded into fighting force, disciplined to productive occupation, and established into a settled, peaceable community. Yet the leader is young, timid, untried. Walking alone, reconnoitering before a most serious encounter, Joshua meets an armed Figure, challenges, and bows in worship: "Put off thy shoes. . . . As commander of the army of the Lord I have now come" (Joshua 5:13f.) .

Worship sets our responsibilities, gifts, weaknesses in perspective of God's commanding of the forces. We are at once humbled to take orders, and exalted as those whom God directs. This the essence of consecration. Worship subdues, arms, and commands for *God's* battles.

C. A keen, politically-minded young courtier, friend of princes, intimate with officers of state and great families, nursing genuine knowledge and concern for his people, with prophet's eye, faith, and concern, attends the funeral service of good, wise, godly king, whose death was at that time a tragedy for Judah. The young man has a deep concern for the nation, harried by strife for position; and knows Uzziah's death a blow against the forces of righteousness. But receives the vision of God — the changeless King enthroned above Judah; he hears the call for men, for true servants of *God,* the *state,* and *righteousness* — always society's need of *men.* Isaiah's impulse is to offer himself, yet he knows himself too involved in the sins of his people to serve a Holy God. "Woe is me. . . ." He is eager to help redeem, but sees himself as needing redemption, as no better than those he thinks of helping! Yet in spite of his confession, the Divine Voice commands, burning ember from altar purges, and he offers himself humbly, penitently, for the immense task of serving as God's spokesman in the turbulent days ahead.

It happened at worship. God found His man — a man with concern, social conscience, personal penitence, utter honesty and obedience (Isaiah 6:1f.).

D. Fourth is Christ Himself, not at worship but echoing the ancient command "Thou shalt worship," in the midst of His own bitter temptation. Come from baptism to think out the future and to plan his ministry, He faces alternatives — a Kingdom by bribery (stones into bread), by spectacle ("cast Thyself down"), or by force (worship the world's ruling force — Satan). Christ refuses all three, replies: "worship . . . serve . . . the Lord thy God." That utter devotion is His central anchorage in testing, His resource for argument ("It is written . . ."), and His fountain of strength ("man *lives* by every word . . . of God"). And angels minister to Him (Matthew 4:1f.).

Worship is nowhere more directly linked with personal temptation and testing. Nowhere is its value as protecting, arming and sustaining more authoritatively declared. In the experience of worship, the man and the methods are prepared for all that God plans to do.

E. The eleven, with probably many others about them, gather at an appointed place to meet the risen Lord — with mingled memories, perplexity, doubts and fears of Jewish and Roman hostility ahead. (Matthew 28:16f.). When Jesus came, all — despite the doubts of some — fall in worship. Immediately, they hear assurance of all power given to Christ, whatever the demand or danger. The whole world is the target-area, all earlier horizons shattered; the task is clarified — "make disciples . . . teaching them to observe all things commanded, baptising them. . . ." And His presence is guaranteed through all the days. The unfinished, still valid commission of the church, linked to the never-withdrawn promise of Companionship, was given at *worship* — where they are always renewed.

F. Finally — at the end of scripture — an old church leader, brave, exiled for Christ's name, looks out from inland prison upon the forces of state and church raging against each other. Roman persecution of a new kind has begun, deliberate, politically-inspired, with devotion to "divine' Emperor the test of political loyalty, and all the efficiency of Roman organization behind it.

Church and faith are in dire peril, and the churches he knows intimately, Ephesus, Smyrna, Thyatira, Laodicea, and the rest, are in no condition to withstand it. Yet he sends to them a marvelous message — of the glory of the Christ they serve (Revelation 1), of the need to correct failures within the churches with a view to overcoming, of victory assured already in heaven, of the coming tribulation and essential safety of saints within it, of the downfall of Rome at last, and of the New City of God to come. And all this has been given him as he falls to worship (Revelation 1:17-19). Worship has imparted vision, the anticipation of victory, an undefeatable confidence in Christ, and the whole church is nerved to prolonged resistance.

Such are the permanent values of worship; it:

A. encourages fresh beginning under divine direction,

B. inspires new consecration with divine enabling,

C. arms genuine social concern with divine pardon and power,

D. rebuts personal temptation with renewed divine resources,

E. kindles world vision with divine commission,

F. renews moral courage with divine assurance.

Whenever men worship, God works.

18. *But God* ...

"But God, who is rich in mercy . . ." — Ephesians 2:4

Introduction

A. A whole philosophy of life lies within that phrase "But God . . ."; the single adversative syllable — *But* — challenges a whole trend of modern thought. Combined with the name of the All-wise, All-mighty Lord, it challenges a basic assumption of our time — the assumption of determination, fatalism, blind omnipotent "fate."

B. "But God" throws the lie in the face of the total philosophy of *the closed circle*.

1. *The world is a closed shop* for the material scientist, economist, Marxist, where self-acting laws determine destiny and all is foreseeable and fixed in grooves of firm necessity.

2. *The soul is a closed sphere* which the psychologist has dissected, analysed, and labeled and which the psychiatrist rules, the racial unconscious controlling the individual unconscious, the individual unconscious controlling the subconscious, the subconscious controlling the conscious — all tabulated, explored, and explained *to* us, not *by* us, until character is a chemical reaction, love is an equation of forces, and free men fighting for freedom in a free Society are deluded automatons whose strings are pulled by destiny.

3. *History becomes a closed series* of cause and effect, action provoking inevitable reaction, pendulum mindlessly swinging, humanity on a tramway car whose course is predetermined by its rails, whose driver is blind.

C. This the comfortable assumption of many in the twentieth century —in part a gesture of defiance against moral responsibility; in part a sigh of despair; in part a shield of indifference and neutralism; in part an alibi for failure.

D. And Christianity cries — "But God . . . !" Neither the world nor soul nor history is closed to God. There is freedom, originality, initiative, at the heart of things — and *anything* can happen.

I. Man conceives a world confused and doomed without God, but God breaks in.

Twice Scripture says this explicitly, but it lies beneath all the Bible's thought.

A. Isaiah 60:1, 2 — darkness covers the earth; thick darkness covers the peoples. A mighty, seemingly invulnerable, pagan empire holds the known world in thralldom — lewd, violent, luxurious, cruel, heathen; its very religion is degrading and corrupt. What hope is there for deliverance? Whence shall come wisdom, morality, freedom, hope? All is dark. *But the Lord* will arise . . . your light has come. Only fools leave God out of their reckoning.

B. Galatians 4: Paul sees the world in still darker terms, as in bondage, slavery to the spirit-world of evil, dominated by demonic forces of ignorance, corruption, division, rebellion, and sin, helpless and doomed because alienated from God. "But when the time had fully come God sent forth His Son . . . to redeem." Always God breaks in, and always to redeem.

C. A young student, disturbed at Orwell's *1984* — picture of world-dictatorship of the most ruthless, inhuman type, as the inevitable outcome of post-war developments — poured out his fears, recounted the wave of cynical pessimism sweeping University campus after wide reading and discussion. Then he met with the firm reminder *"But God...."* The world and the future are God's; always He intervenes. The tide turns at low water as well as high, and the spirit of man has never broken yet. God does not let it. He breaks in. Because it is His world, He can. Because He loves it, He does. And anything can happen. Over the future hangs a question-mark; over the question mark, the throne of God.

II. Christians confront situations forbidding and baffling without God, but God breaks in.

A. At Corinth, the church was divided, in peril, scandals, schism, and selfishness (even at Lord's Table), benighted by self-appointed leaders, sexual license, unbelief (about resurrection), and intellectual pride —everything that could destroy all fruit of the mission to Corinth. Paul's concern silences even his evangelistic zeal (II Corinthians 2:12, 13) and grieves his soul (2:4).

"But God . . . comforted us" (7:5-7) by the total transformation of a "hopeless" situation of which even Paul nearly despaired. God, too, was in Corinth.

B. Paul was sick, weak, hampered, harassed, pleading for healing and release, that he might work unhindered. His prayer went unanswered, though thrice repeated. All seemed mystery, failure, frustration.

But He said to me, "My grace is sufficient. . . . My power is made perfect in weakness." The situation was transformed — made profitable — by the incoming of God *into* it, *not* by the removal of Paul from it (II Corinthians 12)

C. The Philippian church, generous beyond ability, giving more than it could afford to maintain Paul's mission, was itself insecure, in peril of want, even "extreme poverty" (I Corinthians 8:2, 3).

" *'But' my God* shall supply every need" (Philippians 4:19, K.J.V. and Greek — as passage requires). Faith giving so prodigally will not find God faithless.

In this way backsliding, illness, and poverty all yield to divine intervention; *no* situation is hopeless — for God breaks in.

III. Individuals plan careers, careless of the will of God, but God breaks in.

A. The rich farmer in Christ's parable planned increased barns in which to store his goods. Neither work nor wealth, nor success is wrong in itself, but life planned on a wrong sense of values is shortsighted, misled: "Thou fool." God is sovereign: *"but God* said . . . 'This night thy soul. . . .' "

1. *We say* so many things — about plans, hopes, dreams, blueprints for castles in the air.

2. *But God says* — ill-health, accident, failure, unexpected and frustrating responsibilities — and the castles dissolve, the schemes crash.

We forget that we are creatures, not in charge of life, but finding a goal only in obedience to a plan not of our making. James 4:15 is not a needless bit of overscrupulousness ("if the Lord wills, we shall . . ."), but reverent reckoning on the sovereignty of God (Luke 12:16f.).

B. A happier instance involved a young Rabbi, brilliant, zealous, exceptionally well trained, an ardent protagonist of his religion. A whole career of dazzling success was open before him, and his path was clear — as far as Damascas! There God's intervention transformed all the future — gloriously (Acts 9).

Reckon with God as you plan your life and the future; it is right and also wise.

IV. Lives become corrupted, sinful, lost, without God, but God breaks in.

Here psychologists, behaviorists, and sociologists are so often depressing: "all trends are fixed in childhood, all the moulds set, heredity will out, environment controls." Freedom is seen as a chimera, and responsibility a social myth.

A. Paul recalls the character of the Ephesians — the citizens of a city of cultured sin — beauty, art, religion at the service of sensuality. The readers were once *dead* in trespasses and sins, walking the course of the world, subject to demonic evil, possessed by the spirit of disobedience, living for the flesh, pursuing the lusts of body and mind, deserving wrath, victims of a heredity of paganism.

"*But God,* who is rich in mercy . . . love . . . made us alive together with Christ . . . raised us up with Him. . . ." The evil entail is broken, the vicious circle snapped and entered by the saving grace of God (Ephesians 2:1-6).

B. Paul recalls the character of the Corinthians — people of a city of uncultured sin — a seaport, commercial, cosmopolitan, corrupt. "Corinthian" was a by-word for vice, an epithet actionable in the courts as slander. Some of Paul's readers had been immoral, idolaters, adulterers, homosexuals, thieves, gluttons, drunkards, revilers, robbers, victims of an environment of viciousness.

But they were washed, sanctified, justified in the name of Jesus — set in new environment "in Christ," because God in mercy broke in (I Corinthians 6:9-11).

C. The last word on this is Christ's. Speaking of the problems of the rich in entering the kingdom, as a promising young candidate for discipleship turned away, Jesus shocked the Twelve with an emphasis on the difficulty of change and met their despairing "who then can be saved?" with a final, authoritative *"But God"* — "with men, impossible, *but with God* all things are possible."

19. *Prophecy of Pentecost*

"This is what was spoken by the prophet Joel: 'And in the last days it shall be, God declares, that I will pour out My Spirit upon all flesh, and your sons and your daughters shall prophesy, and your young men shall see visions and your old men shall dream dreams; yea, and on my menservants and my maidservants in those days I will pour out my Spirit; and they shall prophesy'" — Acts 2:16-18

Introduction

A. Peter's explanation of Pentecost is almost as surprising as the experience itself. Wind, flame, and gift of tongues were outward *signs* of prodigious event. Sudden and overwhelming transformation of the men — from fear to boldness, from silence to eloquence, from discretion to accusation, from perplexity to intoxication, from passivity to aggression — is the essential *content,* together with deeper delayed effects in the church and in the characters of believers. Peter's *explanation* of the event borrows the obscure words of Joel, seemingly less apposite than certain words of Ezekiel (36:26; 37:1-14) or Isaiah (61:1-4) or John the Baptist — popularly accepted as a prophet (Matthew 3:11). Yet, on examination, Joel's words prove most pertinent of all.

B. Joel was one of the five men who labored at different times and by different means to rebuild Judah after the Exile — Nehemiah by physical reconstruction, Zechariah by prophecy, Haggai by Temple-building, Ezra by re-education in Law, Joel by calling for repentance and a new spirit. Joel's was the deepest analysis of the nation's need — including the loftiest conception of blessing to be given, the most daring of all prophecies of restoration: the outpouring of God's Spirit. Only so could Judah find her soul and fulfill her destiny; the city, the temple, the education would be useless otherwise.

C. Peter likewise analyzes the real need of Judaism — not deliverance from Rome, or an apocalyptic Messiah, or a kingdom of Zealots, but regeneration. Political independence and religious nationalism were delusions. A kingdom of the spirit, such as Jesus preached, was the real solution Israel sought — a new heart and spirit, the kingdom within, the way of Jesus — the Christ. And this, as Joel had said, could be achieved only by the Spirit from on high. This had now happened.

D. Moreover the words of Joel provided *evidence* that Peter spoke truth — *tests* which hearers could apply. For Joel named the essential marks of the divine outpouring, the national regeneration. It would be recognized by:

I. The Reversal of the Established Order

A. Joel signalized this in images of violent reversals in nature — the sun becomes darkness, the moon reddens to blood, columns of fire and smoke appear — eclipses, eruptions, convulsions; for the spiritual order invades the natural and result is upheaval. This explains the miracles attendant upon Christ's mission, and apostolic church, especially the resurrection of Christ. The divine world invaded.

B. So socially, too. The aged remain young — dream; the young have insights, the wisdom of aged; servants share with masters (Joel means "the" menservants, maidservants) ; females share with males; sons and daughters are alike. Old distinctions are swept away in the kingdom of Christ. Reversals foreseen in the Song of Mary ("put down mighty, exalted humble and meek, satisfied poor, rich sent empty away" — Luke 1:46f.) and proclaimed by Jesus ("First shall be last, last first"; and in parable of Rich Man and Lazarus) are due to the Spirit "blowing where it will." Harlots precede Scribes into the Kingdom; old men are born again; the foolish shame the wise; the weak shame the strong; what is low, despised, and non-existent is chosen to bring to nothing "what is" (I Corinthians 1:27). What is exalted among men is an abomination in the sight of God. The Gentiles' "great ones" lord it over men, but among Christ's disciples, he who would be great must be *servant* of all. Revelation is made to "babes"; apostles "turn the world upside down" — all signs of intervention by the regenerating, renewing Spirit of God. As Joel foresaw, revolution, not evolution, would mark the Day of the Lord.

II. The Universalizing of What Had Been Exceptional

A. Vision, dream, and prophesying had been confined to special persons, chosen of God. *They* had Spirit, were in God's counsel, and possessed God's secrets (e.g., Jeremiah 23:21, 22). So the Spirit was believed to confer superhuman gifts, powers, and experiences, for a brief time and for limited purposes, upon certain individuals. The skill, wisdom, courage, and strength of artists, craftsmen, poets, soldiers, local prodigies like Samson are so explained (Exodus 31:3; Numbers 11:26; 24:2; 27:18; Judges 13:25; 14:6, 19; 15:14). Always the gift and manifestation of the Spirit of God was *exceptional*.

B. Yet it was promised that "all the Lord's people shall be prophets," "all shall know me from least to greatest, none need teach his neighbour" (Jeremiah 31:34; cf. Numbers 11:29). All shall be in God's counsels — old, young, sons, daughters, servants shall be prophets, seers, dreamers. The divine democracy shall be fulfilled — all shall be one in Christ Jesus. There shall be a leveling-up in privilege, opportunity, experience of God (not necessarily in ability, authority, responsibility): all shall know God and enter His presence.

C. This is manifest in the apostolic Church — an élite of *laymen* — fishers and taxmen, unlearned and unlettered men of the people — "people of the earth" whom Caiaphas pronounced "accursed." This offended both the religious caste of Judaism and the sages of Greece, but it is a sign of the Spirit. The exceptional is universalized; the "nest of consecrated cobblers," as a critic called the earliest Missionary society — the "common rabble," as Wesley's hearers were regarded, receive the Spirit of God and confound the mighty. Impulsive, panic-stricken, Christ-denying Peter, now confronting all Jerusalem, is a living illustration of the point.

III. The Extension of Horizons to the Uttermost

"Whosoever shall call upon the name of the Lord shall be saved."

A. It is sometimes argued that Joel thought only of Israel. "All flesh," suggesting "all humanity," seems certainly wide; and "whosoever shall call on the name" seems universal. So Peter applied the words "to all afar off, as many as the Lord . . . shall call." The exclusive election is ended: *all may be saved — the widest possible scope,* by the *surest possible promise,* on *simplest possible terms.* No limitation, of grace or invitation or love, is ever born of God's universal Spirit. Where that Spirit rules, the world is the target. Endued with power from on high, though we "begin at Jerusalem," we head for the "uttermost parts of the world."

B. This again became evident in the life of the apostolic church. A sharp break with Judaism came with Paul's world-mission, the admission of Gentiles, and the universalism of salvation by faith in Christ alone. Though the church herself took long to grasp and act upon it, this is a sure sign of the presence of the Spirit — always. A Spirit-born revival always begets Missions.

Such signs of the Spirit, foreseen by Joel and confirmed by Peter, are timelessly valid:

1. reversal of established "natural" order,
2. universalising of "exceptional" privilege,
3. extension of spiritual horizons.

How we still need Pentecost, in precisely these manifestations!

20. Not By Might . . .

"This is the word of the Lord to Zerubbabel: not by might, nor by power, but by my Spirit, says the Lord of hosts" — Zechariah 4:6

Introduction

If ever a simple, popular story symbolized a nation's faith, "David and Goliath" does: a shepherd boy against an experienced warrior, five smooth pebbles against helmet of brass and spear like weaver's beam. The Lord was with *David,* and *the little man won* (I Samuel 18) .

I. But that is Israel's story — the story of little people, a small nation amid mighty empires — Egypt, Assyria, Babylon, Persia, Greece, Rome, then Europe down to Hitler. Always "David" endures, undefeated though suffering.

A. The theme runs through all her history: always, the race not to the swift nor the battle to the strong (Ecclesiastes 9:11) .

1. Moses vs. Pharaoh (hosts, riders, chariots lost — Exodus 14);

2. Joshua vs. Jericho (no blow struck — Joshua 6) ;

3. Gideon and his valiant three hundred vs. the Midianite hordes (Judges 7:4f.) .

Always the few with God are mighty (Isaiah 60:22) .

B. *King Asa* declares: "It is nothing with God to save by many or by few." *King Jehoshaphat*: "Be not dismayed at this great multitude. The battle is not yours but God's." *Prophet Elijah* reads God's commentary on contemporary events — the violence and bluster of Ahab's reign: "The Lord not in earthquake . . . wind . . . fire: but in still small voice . . ." (II Chronicles 14:11; 20:15; I Kings 19:9f.) .

C. *Hezekiah* saw the David - Goliath situation enacted before his eyes. Sennacherib's mighty host invested the city, shutting up Judah "like a bird in a cage," all the might of giant Assyria confronting one small, sparsely defended, ill-supplied, friendless city. But the seige was lifted overnight, and the city was miraculously delivered. (II Kings 18:13-19:37) . The Psalmist dramatically represents this divine victory:

> *The heathen raged; the Kingdoms were moved*:
> *He uttered His voice —*
> *The earth melted!* (Psalm 46:6)

The stars in their courses fight for God's people (Judges 5:20f.), and faith proves mightier than the sword.

II. So comes the promise to Zerubbabel.

A. Zerubbabel, the leader among returning exiles, was a descendant of David, indicated by Zechariah and Haggai as divinely appointed to rebuild, probably held by some as "Messiah." Certainly he was the hope of his time.

B. Yet the situation he faced was forbidding, overwhelming, "impossible":

1. *To rebuild a nation-state,* in a still ruined land, with a few disheartened, disunited people, poor, struggling, reluctant, and amid foes;

2. *To rekindle faith* after exile, adversity, high hopes frustrated, and great visions of glorious homecoming disappointed — with Persia, the mighty heathen overlord, still firmly in control of Judah's destiny;

3. *To re-establish the Temple* and all it represented, when food, materials, houses, labor, and money were very scarce; and the people had little heart for old ways and worship that had failed them.

C. And the resources were negligible: Zerubbabel possessed neither the authority nor the consent of Persia, nor the means of defense. Judah had lived long under despotic military dictatorship, where authority, power, and compulsion got things done; and military prowess upheld a tyrannical throne, embodying executive omnipotence.

Against this, Judah was puny, Zerubbabel helpless, the tasks impossible.

D. Hence the wording of the promise: the swift, mighty multitude of well armed giants is *not* strong against God's David. *Not* by compulsive power of human authority and direction, *not* by weight of armies, force of arms, threats of vengeance, but by *My Spirit* — the still small voice, the secret, inward influence that liberates unseen forces and brings hidden factors into play, so shall the State, faith, worship, and the future be rebuilt: and Judah's life shall begin again "by my Spirit."

III. So comes the Promise to us.

Is not this precisely parallel to the impossible, overwhelming situation facing the Eleven before Pentecost? In Caesar's world, Jewry was hostile, and not many wise, noble, or mighty were among the believers: Jesus was "gone" — all the future seemed forbidding:
Then came the Spirit:

A. *Challenging them to believe in new beginnings,* despite all appearances; with God the prospect is never hopeless;

B. *Challenging them to believe in the rebuilding of the Church,* the return to worship, revival of true religion, re-awakening of desire, re-kindling of repentance, which the Spirit can still effect;

C. *Challenging them to believe in the future,* for the Spirit will never be withdrawn, and tomorrow is God's.

We lack all outward signs of worldly success and victory — as did Zerubbabel — but we have the Spirit. The Promise *still* is ours.

21. *Missionary Directive*

"The Gospel must first be preached to all nations" — Mark 13:10

Introduction

Chapter of trouble: wars, followed by famine, disaster (vv. 7, 8); treachery, insubordination, break-up of homes, unreasoning hatreds (vv. 12, 13); religious faction, persecution by State, opposition by popular feeling (vv. 9, 13); multifarious new cults, "isms," pseudo-religions with demonic power, specious promises (vv. 5-6, 21-22). A catalogue of tribulations, like morning paper: troubles political, economic, moral, social, domestic, and religious — all at once. Pessimism unlimited; utopia debunked, a sociologist's nightmare; ample justification for inactivity. A world going to the devil — nothing one can do! Yet here, Jesus says, is the —

I. Context of Mission

Right in the middle of opposition, decay, persecution, and heresy is the missionary directive (v. 10). When everything about you is going wrong, evangelize the world! When reason piles on reason for entrenchment, digging in, cutting down, economizing — send forth the gospel. Trouble is the *normal* context of missionary challenge.

The world has seen three creative moments for world-evangelization, each set against background of commotion, upheaval:

A. There was deep unrest, extensive migrations, clash and conflict of cultures, when Abram left Ur of the Chaldees, some 4,000 years ago, to seek religious freedom and opportunity in new land. All the Middle East was in upheaval: "Not the time for spiritual ventures!"

Yet out of that situation came the world-faith of Judaism, the divine preparation for Christ.

B. The outlook was bleak, forbidding; Caesar's empire was securely established, Jewish and Roman reactions fanatically hostile. The recent crucifixion of Christ was no augury of welcome or success for the Christian way of life: "Not the time for spiritual ventures!"

Yet out of that situation came the command of Jesus on the Mount above Bethany and the first world-expansion of the Church.

C. War drums were throbbing throughout England, Russia, France, Germany, Turkey, Poland, barely silenced in America, when Carey set sail for India to initiate modern movement of organized Church-based missions: "Surely not the time for spiritual ventures!"

D. So in these last sixty chaotic years *we* have seen the beginnings of a vast new movement towards a truly international church consciousness and a return to Biblical theology — though we complain this is not an age of faith. The ancient idea that divine activity is ever accompanied by darkness, tempest, floods, earthquakes, and war is symbolic: God always initiates His new enterprises in the darkest hour, when holy places are beseiged, prophets in prison, believing hearts despondent. The troubled, frightened, chaotic unpromising time has ever been the time for missionary expansion; excuses for postponement, inactivity are really incentives for enterprise.

E. Today, the resurgence of nationalism in Asia and Africa, the sharpening of racial problems throughout world, the rapid infiltrations of Communism, the closing of China, Tibet, and Ceylon, the secularization of India, persecution in Russia, Colombia, and Spain, the strong revival of Hinduism, Buddhism, and Islam, world conditions that play havoc with mission-board finance, the demand for ever higher qualifications for missionaries in India and the Congo, the rising of shallow, self-centered revivalism at home — all these present disheartening conditions. But the worse the time, the clearer Christ's call; we redeem the *time because* the days are evil. The *right* time never comes. Every time is appropriate for evangelistic outreach. The worse the time, the more appropriate it is. Trouble is the *appointed* context of mission.

This circumstance illumines, secondly —

II. The Compulsion of Mission

"The Gospel must . . . be preached" — both prophecy and command.

A. Frequently *compassion* motivates mission. Peter went to Joppa, Paul to Macedonia, to *"help."* Compassion towards slaves in a Roman market-place took Augustine to England. And the same Christ-inspired love towards the leper — the blind, ignorant, hungry, dying, sinful, and lost, still drives many to go and serve, teach, heal, tell.

B. Sometimes *persecution* has motivated mission — as when the disciples were scattered from Jerusalem by persecution arising about Stephen, as when the Pilgrim Fathers found refuge and opportunity in America, as in the case of the Huguenots in England, the Chinese (from sea-board) in Inner China — always taking the Gospel. God sometimes stirs up the nest!

C. Occasionally *investment* motivates mission. Pearce Carey writes of eighteenth-century England: "that century of reaction, when the mercury fell low, reason clipped faith's wings, enthusiasm was a reproach, and religion icily regular," when the critics held the field, and

Hume was the oracle and Voltaire, "that Philistine of transcendent cleverness" was the idol, when Gibbon was subjecting the warm wonder of the first Christian centuries to cool analysis, and "all people of discernment had discovered Christianity to be fictitious"; and of the churches, "lifelessness, sparse worshippers, coarse choristers, neglected parishes, Sabbath drink-revels, spent enthusiasms, barren and bitter disputations, bitterness and lowness of ideal and life."

At such time, what better to do with the rich treasure of the Gospel than send it to those who never received it, to cherish, explore and enjoy, preserving by propagating; to receive again with interest?

D. Often *vision* motivates mission. Vision of the world redeemed, Christ's way universally followed. Placing side by side two incontrovertible convictions — the kind of world-order Christians want must be world-wide, and the kind of world-order Christians want must have spiritual foundations — makes the missionary imperative unanswerable. As there can be no island of peace in a world at war, or of prosperity in a world of poverty, so there can be no secure island of faith in a world of unbelief; the conception of a privileged, self-centered group, content to save themselves is *unchristian*. Christ's vision of the *world* as God's kingdom is binding on us all.

E. Yet the deepest motivation of all is Christ's *command*. Paul, Carey, Livingstone, Judson, Gilmour — and hundreds more felt *compulsion*. Hence, the nature of the time, the prospects of success, the risk of rejection, the probability of death are *irrelevant*. Plain as the command to "follow," to baptism, to the Lord's Supper, and to love one another, was the command to "go, make disciples." The Gospel *must* be preached — so the disciple must go and preach it. The inner logic of the Christian faith, enshrined in scripture, here narrows to a personal direct injunction which demands obedience. To plead circumstances, or unfitness, may be mere evasion; to argue that "the world cannot be bettered till Jesus comes" is to twist Christ's teaching into an excuse for ignoring His command!

The compulsion holds: it drove St. Paul west, Carey east, Livingstone south, Grenfell north: has it moved us — even to next door?

22. End — and Beginning

"He led them out as far as Bethany, and lifting up his hands he blessed them. While he blessed them, he parted from them" — Luke 24:50, 51

Introduction

A. Bethany is barely five straight miles from Bethlehem, perhaps seven and a half by road. Yet between Bethlehem's Advent and Bethany's Ascension stretches the epoch comprising the life, ministry, death, and resurrection of Jesus.

B. Though they are so different, the two events correspond. As heaven attested Christ's Birth, through prophets, angels, and saints, so at His Ascension all power in heaven was given unto Him. As men worshipped at the cradle though Herod threatened, so men worshipped at the Ascension though some doubted. As the Babe was hailed "Immanuel — God with us," so the ascending Lord undertook to remain "with us" always. The world attended His coming, and the world attends His leaving. All roads — of prophecy, shepherds, wise men, the Roman census — had led to Bethlehem; now all roads led out from Bethany — to Jerusalem, Judea. Samaria, to all nations, to the uttermost parts of earth. Bethlehem and Bethany join hands in one gracious saying: "As the Father has sent me, even so send I you" (John 20:21).

C. Approached this way, from Bethlehem, the Ascension at Bethany is seen plainly to be:

I. The Fittest Close to Christ's Earthly Ministry

It is hard indeed to imagine any other end:

A. *Return*: "He came from God, and went to God"; "descended . . . ascended"; "took upon Him the form of servant, humbled himself, even to death — the death of the cross — wherefore God exalted him" (John 13:3; Ephesians 4:9; Philippians 2:7-9). Repeatedly it is said He "came," "was sent," "was manifested" — implying His personal pre-existence. The Ascension completes the Incarnation, as He who "came from the Father . . . into the world . . ." is seen "leaving the world and going to the Father" (John 16:28). How else could Advent close but with Return?

B. *Vindication*: Always in the New Testament the power by which Christ rose and ascended is ascribed to God. God vindicated Christ — His claims, teaching, passion, and death. In the triumph of Easter and the glory of Ascension, all apparent failure was eclipsed in victory, all weakness and humiliation forgotten in glory. Men lifted Christ to die upon the cross, rejected, but God raised Him to the skies to reign, exalted:

> *The Head that once was crowned with thorns*
> *Is crowned with glory now;*
> *A royal diadem adorns*
> *The mighty Victor's brow.*

C. *Seal*: "on him has God the Father set his seal" (John 6:27). Paul keeps the death and resurrection of Jesus in closest connection — "we believe Jesus died and rose again . . . delivered for our offenses, raised . . . for justification. . . . Christ died according to the scriptures . . . rose according to the scriptures . . . . unto Him who died and was raised . . . If Christ be not *raised* . . . ye are yet in your sins" (I Thessalonians 4:14; Romans 4:25; I Corinthians 15:3f.; II Corinthians 5:15; I Corinthians 15:17). Ascension takes its place, with baptism and Transfiguration, in a threefold divine attestation to Jesus, answering Christ's "It is finished" with God's "It is accepted."

D. *Enthronement*: Christ came as the prophesied King of David's line. Born King, he was so welcomed by the Magi; he promised in parable and prophecy to "sit on the throne of His glory." What more necessary end of the story than that He should sit at "right hand of Majesty on high"? (Hebrews 1:3). God rewarded His "self-emptying" by conferring on Him a name above every name, at which every knee must bend (Philippians 2:9-11). "We see Jesus" (already) regnant — on Ascension Day (Hebrews 2:9) "crowned with glory and honour."

E. *Blessing*: Peter movingly summarizes the purpose of Christ's coming "God . . . sent him . . . to bless you" (Acts 3:26). Countless suppliants, sick, sinful, and friendless, found it true. No final picture of Jesus *could* be more fitting — standing, hands upraised in blessing, gathering into final benediction upon His own all the grace, gifts, and benefits His ministry and death conferred. The whole gospel of grace culminates in that gesture of Savior's goodwill.

So the greatest story in the world ends greatly, so far as it has ever ended. Return, vindication, sealing, enthronement, blessing are in the last words of the gospel record, and these must be central themes in our evangel *and in our faith*.

Nevertheless, the Ascension at Bethany is just as plainly:

II. A Wonderful Beginning to the Church's World Career

The activity ascribed to our ascended Lord is the background of the activity and experience of the Church on earth. The figure of Christ ascending merges into that of:

A. *Christ working*: "They went forth and preached everywhere, the Lord worked with them, and confirmed message by signs" is now the ending of Mark's Gospel. Luke begins his account of the Church's life with a reference to all that Jesus "began" to do, implying that Christ's work continued in the work of the apostles; so Luke explains crucial events — the release of Peter, the conversion of Cornelius and of Saul, the direction of Paul to Macedonia. Christian workers are servants — tools — of an ascended Lord:

> For the garden tomb is empty and the East
> is silver grey
> As the angels of the Morning trumpet in
> another day:
> See the wounded God go walking down the
> world's eternal way
> For His task is never done.

B. *Christ endowing*: "Being . . . exalted at the right hand of God . . . he has poured out this . . ." (Acts 2:33). "When He ascended . . .

gave gifts unto men . . . that some should be apostles . . . prophets . . . evangelists . . . pastors . . . teachers . . ." (Ephesians 4:8-11). The *figure* is of a Roman general distributing gifts in celebration of triumph. The *experience* is of power, wisdom, words, courage, results, beyond all one's resources or deserving, given at the moment of need for effective service. The ascended Lord *equips* His disciples for diligent work.

C. *Christ interceding*: "We have Advocate with the Father" (I John 2:1); "Christ Jesus . . . at right hand of God . . . intercedes for us" (Romans 8:34); "Christ has entered . . . heaven itself . . . now to appear in presence of God on our behalf. . . . We have a great High Priest . . . always lives to make intercession . . ." (Hebrews 10:24; 4:14; 7:25). The imagination is baffled, of course, but Jesus is certainly the High Priest of Humanity. The cross has an eternal dimension, an endless efficacy. The ascended Lord pleads His sacrifice continually for our continuing sin.

D. *Christ receiving*: "I go to prepare a place for you . . . . I will take you to myself" (John 14:2, 3).

> More homelike seems the vast unknown
> Since Thou hast entered there . . .

Death, to Paul, is simply "to be with Christ . . . far better" (Philippians 1:23). Seven times Christ is said to "sit" at God's right hand, but Stephen, in his moment of death, saw Him "standing" as though to receive His own (Acts 7:55). The ascended Christ is our forerunner within the veil (Hebrews 6:20) — a personal Friend in courts of heaven.

E. *Christ coming*: "I will come again . . . this Jesus, who was taken up from you into heaven, will come in the same way . . . *when* Christ, who is our life, appears . . . we await a Saviour, the Lord Jesus . . ." (John 14:3; Acts 1:11; Colossians 3:4; Philippians 3:20). The ascended Lord awaits God's time (Hebrews 10:13) and the consummation of the age.

In this realm, scripture's vision far outreaches ours. We can only meditate upon the pictures offered, but the fivefold Ascension faith with which the apostolic Church confronted her task is clear: Christ *working* beside her, *endowing* her leaders, *interceding* for her failures, *receiving* her dead, *coming* in glory.

No wonder she triumphed!

23. *The Fullness of God*

"That you may be filled with all the fullness of God" — Ephesians 3:19

Introduction

A. A wonderful phrase, "the fullness of God": something of a slogan, catch-phrase, in Greek thought. The Greeks thought of a vast gulf stretching between pure, eternal spirit and mere temporal matter (somewhat as we think of vast space surrounding the earth, pierced by radio-telescopes and astronauts) and filling the gulf countless gradations of spiritual beings forming a descending "chain" of spiritual *de*volution, each little less pure than the one above it: the total chain was "fullness." Paul repeatedly insists that Christ fills that gulf, is Himself that *fullness*, bridges the distance between God and man.

B. The Hebrews, as usual, had a more concrete, picturesque usage. They spoke of the "fullness" of the earth, meaning its infinite, teeming variety of creatures (Psalm 24:1), and of the "fullness" of the sea, meaning its unfathomable depth and mystery (Psalm 96:11). Sometimes, the word was popularly used to refer to the full cargo of a laden vessel.

C. All this immensity of meaning and association is in the phrase. God fills every void, spans every space. In Christ He descended and ascended that He might fill all (Ephesians 4:10). God's greatness embraces the infinite variousness of all living things, a sea-depth of riches, wisdom, knowledge, unsearchable judgments, inscrutable ways (Romans 11:33), a laden treasure-ship of grace, mercy, truth, and goodwill.

> *O Love of God, how strong and true*
> *Eternal, and yet ever new;*
> *Uncomprehended and unbought,*
> *Beyond all knowledge and all thought.*
>
> *O Love of God, how deep and great!*
> *Far deeper than man's deepest hate;*
> *Self-fed, self-kindled like the light,*
> *Changeless, eternal, infinite.*

Nevertheless, this uncomprehended, immeasurable fullness of God is:

I. Explored and Expounded in Apostolic Faith

A. God's fullness was *explored* in the developing experience of convert after convert, as each knew God:

1. first, as Creator of the world, Almighty Spirit, "Father of gods and men" or some other guise;

2. then, in Christ, as human, incarnate, near, but self-evidently divine;

3. finally, as Spirit at Pentecost and in the Spirit-filled life of the Christian community. Each disciple passed through this mind-stretching discipline, confronted with the greatness, richness, and depth of God in *fact* and *life,* before defining in words.

B. God's fullness was *expounded* in the threefold name. God is:
1. *Father* — Creator, Sovereign; Source of all power, wisdom, love; Holy, Glorious, in essence Unknowable yet Home of our spirits;
2. *Son* — Redeemer, Mediator, Lord, Example, Priest, Sacrifice, and Friend;
3. *Spirit* — Fountain of holiness, power, and joy, Teacher, Guide Comforter, and indwelling Companion.

Theology is ever the transcript of experience, and the language of worship is the overflow of faith rejoicing in its discoveries. Father-Son-Spirit is the fullness of God spelled out in human terms because learned in human life.

II. Expressed and Exemplified in Apostolic Practice

A. *In the threefold Name converts were baptized,* because the love of God the Father, the grace of Christ the Son, and the ministry of the Spirit were necessary to bring man to salvation (Matthew 28:19).

B. *In the three-fold Name believers worshipped,* drawing near to God the Father, through Christ the Son, in the inspiration and enlightenment of the Spirit: "Through Christ we . . . have access in one Spirit unto the Father" (Ephesians 2:18) is the ruling principle of Christian worship.

C. *In the three-fold Name Christians were blessed.* "The grace of the Lord Jesus Christ, the love of God and the fellowship of the Holy Spirit be with you all" (II Corinthians 13:14) is becoming a familiar benediction not simply at dismissal but in Christian fellowship and family. By such simple repeated practice, the fullness of God was recalled innumerable times in Christian life.

D. In consequence, all that had to do with God grew larger in their eyes, as sharing that fullness. Paul speaks of going to Rome in the fullness of the blessing of the *gospel* of Christ — a message offering plenitude of peace, salvation, power, and joy, telling of the fullness of God. In *Christ,* too, "all the fullness of God was pleased to dwell . . . in Him the whole fullness of deity dwells bodily" (Colossians 1:19; 2:9) — explaining the inexhaustible riches of Christ for those who love Him. And "the fullness of the stature of Christ," morally, becomes our highest ideal (Ephesians 4:13), as that beyond which human aspiration cannot conceive a higher. In some scarcely conceivable way, even the *Church* is seen as "His body, the fullness of Him which filleth all in all" (Ephesians 1:23), as in some sense the complement of the ascended Lord, in God's plan of world redemption.

Gospel, Christ, and Church thus partake of the fullness of God, as this was constantly kept before minds of apostolic believers.

Yet, even all this is but background to the immeasurable richness of daily Christian life, as the fullness of God was:

III. Extolled and Extended in Apostolic Counsel

A. Believers themselves partake of God's infinite richness. Paul declares that all fullness of deity dwells in Christ, and immediately adds "and you have come to fullness of life in Him" (Colossians 2:10). John similarly declares that "from His fullness have we all received, grace upon grace" — as wave after wave of the divine sea of graciousness washes across our lives.

And it is for this that Paul prays on behalf of the Ephesians (3:19). In part, no doubt, he would include "strengthened with might through His Spirit, Christ dwelling in the heart through faith, being rooted and grounded in love, and comprehending the breadth, length, depth, and height of that love": for it must take the whole of man's spiritual nature to receive the fullness of God. But yet *this is the crowning gift* and possibility — a nature so open to God as to receive and possess and transmit, not some niggardly shallow experience of the divine, not some limited, measured list of small-time evangelical "experiences," but all that Christians mean by Father-Son-Spirit.

B. So Trinity Festival reminds of immense ranges of Christian thought and experience beyond usual conceptions of "religious life," above average experience. It beckons us upward, and deeper, till we too possess *the fullness of God.*

24. *Be Strong!*

A Young People's Sermon.

"Lift your drooping hands and strengthen your weak knees, and make straight paths for your feet, so that what is lame may not be put out of joint but rather be healed" — Hebrews 12:12-13

I. These Hebrew Christians learning a lesson very few of us like to learn: nothing, *nothing at all,* can make up for being weak.

A. They were exceptionally *intelligent* and well-informed. The letter to them is learned, argumentative, assumes a great deal of knowledge, especially the history and religion of the Old Testament. The Hebrew Christians were no fools!

B. They were *privileged* with first class Christian teachers, who had heard Christ Himself and were filled with Holy Spirit (2:3-4).

C. They had a wonderful, exciting *conversion* — like a great light breaking into darkness, a great feast of good things, a share in God's Spirit, an introduction to a whole new spiritual world (6:4, 5).

D. They had *begun discipleship extremely well* — with a hard struggle, abused, robbed, fined, some imprisoned — standing up to it bravely (10:32-34).

E. Yet, despite everything, they were running into trouble: some drifting away (2:1); some in danger of slipping back to unbelief, hardened hearts, failure (2:7, 12; 4:1, 2); some "drawing back" from front line, afraid of more persecution (10:39; 12:4). Throughout, the writer calls them to hold fast, not to throw away their confidence, to hold to their first faith, to endure (10:23, 35, 36; 3:14; 4:11; 12:3, 7, 15, 25, etc.).

F. What had gone wrong? It was not easy to be a Jewish Christian — excluded, ostracised, disinherited, often banned from family, treated as traitors; besides being disappointed, perplexed by the overthrow of Palestine and (probably) by the destruction of Jerusalem. But none of this would so badly upset them except for *some want of inner strength*.

Brains, privileges, great experiences, and fine enthusiastic beginnings get nowhere without *strength of character*.

1. A *sportsman* — well coached, in good team, with fine equipment, grounds, health, and plenty of practice — fails if, when things are going badly, he has no inner strength to hold on, play well, never give in. That perseverance needs character.

2. Even if a *student* is in a fine college, with excellent tutors, books, opportunities, friendships, and everything to encourage, his success will turn upon his grit, his ability to stick at his books and research, even when discouraged, distracted, tempted away. There is no high attainment intellectually without strength of character.

3. Painters, musicians, thinkers, writers, and scientists need it no less than do statesmen, soldiers, missionaries, and explorers: tenacity of mind, doggedness of purpose, steadfastness of will, self-dicipline of mood and emotion, and deep, spiritual resources of courage, endurance, firmness. Without the strength that sees clearly and holds on, nothing great is ever achieved. Though we moderns do not like the idea, there is *no* substitute for strength.

Greatness, indeed, *is* strength of character, shining through achievement, endurance, resistance, or suffering.

II. But what is the use of *telling* people to be strong?

A. To be sure, this writer did more. He reminded of all the great, strong men of the past; he recalled the absolute faithfulness of God's promises; he told how Jesus had suffered and resisted, was tempted and understood man's struggles; he reminded of older stories of great beginnings that came to failure through weakness; he warned of the serious consequences of giving in. Could he do more to make them *want* to be strong?

B. But how? Right at the end of his letter he gives simple directions:

1. *"Lift your drooping hands"* — DO SOMETHING!

   a. *Noah,* in time of great wickedness, vexed at the state of society, preached and protested (II Peter 2:5, 8). Although he was one of a tiny minority, he did something as an example, a warning, a concrete expression of his faith in God's judgment. He built a ship.

   b. *Gideon,* hiding behind the winepress, inactive but petulant, complaining of weakness of Israel (and God) before the Midianites, is commanded to go and take action. He cuts down an idol grove, raises a fighting force, and finds the strength of God still with Israel (Judges 6:11-35). At first pleading weakness, he comes to despise it (cf. 6:15; 7:3).

   c. *Nehemiah,* grieved for the destruction of Jerusalem and the exile of Judah; alone, timid, beset by foes and intrigue, praying for God to restore, builds a wall which becomes the bulwark of new faith and the foundation of a new State.

   d. These men were not strong beforehand: *you grow strong by doing,* not by dreaming or wishing or complaining. If your hands are weak, withered, "stretch them forth" — find them strong (Mark 3:1-5). Drooping, idle hands are always weak.

2. *"Strengthen your weak knees"* — STAND FOR SOMETHING!

   There is no illustration in the world like the story of Daniel and his friends:

   a. The Jews were in heathen Babylon, surrounded by idolatry, lewdness, and cruelty; and, as they prospered, by jealousy, plots, and intrigue. His enemies knew Daniel's staunch faith — "no ground of complaint" except concerning the law of his God (Daniel 6:5). Hence they persuaded the proud and foolish king to forbid prayers. But Daniel continued "as previously" (6:10), unmoved, unafraid. Standing for God he *stood,* unbowed. And enemies proved helpless.

   b. The three friends, similarly, were cornered by an edict to worship the King's image. They refused, believing God would deliver them, *"But if not . . . we will not serve your gods"* (Daniel 3:1-18). To the resistance of men like these, Judah owed her survival, and we owe much of our faith.

   c. So with Luther, Lincoln, Churchill — *what you stand for makes you strong.*

3. *"Make straight paths for your feet"* — LEAD SOMEWHERE!

   a. The heroes of Jewish youth were not all fighters, reformers, resisters. The Jews honored especially the pioneers and pilgrim-explorers who broke new frontiers, opened up new lands, enlarged horizons — Abraham, not knowing whither but journeying on; Isaac, Jacob, Moses the intrepid leader of migration, are all mentioned in Hebrews 11. In their tracks, Paul the dauntless traveler, Marco Polo, Columbus, Cortez, Livingstone, Amundsen, Scott — men with strength to see far, to dare peril, and to keep on — not to follow the crowd, but to lead.

b. That is why the path must be "straight," so that lame, weaker followers may not stumble. Welsh mountain streams in winter are swollen to sudden torrents by rain, storms, and melting snow; they drown thousands of young lambs, because the ewes will leap to upland ravines, and the lambs seeking to follow are swept away. There are always others looking to us — younger brothers, sisters, schoolmates, colleagues, friends. Do we pioneer straight, safe paths for ourselves and them? or do we lead astray?

c. Beautifully, this letter calls Jesus "Pioneer" (File-Leader) — (12:2).

These are the kinds of strength that *really* matter: achievement, principle, leadership. We grow strong by doing, standing, setting out straight, looking unto Jesus.

Be Strong!

25. *Things that Constitute Salvation*

"Now that you have been set free from sin and have become slaves of God, the return you get is sanctification and its end, eternal life" — Romans 6:22

Introduction

A. Interesting how many of Paul's sentences read like sermon outlines, not merely because many sermons are preached on them, but because Paul has preacher's love of pithy summaries, thumb-nail analyses of great themes, packing into single statements fruits of long thinking and rich, authoritative understanding.

B. So this text is a portmanteau utterance, a condensed "formula" of individual salvation, the quintessence of evangelical truth. The key word "now"; it contrasts past and present, life as it was, life as it is now with Christ. What difference does Christ make? What *is* "salvation"?

I. Salvation comprises a certain experience — liberation: "You have been set free from sin (though not free "of" sin!).

A. The clue is in the foregoing expressions — servitude, slavery, obedience, reigning, dominion (vv. 6, 9, 12, 14, 16, 17). These terms would be exaggerations, if the passage were not strictly autobiographical.

Chapter 7 explains them, recalling the experience of *wanting* to do good, and failing; wanting to avoid evil, and falling. Paul tells of his high ideals of home, tradition, training and religion, failing to control his strong, passionate, rebellious nature. Education and inspiration are not enough; *an inner bondage* of temptation, habit, imagination, and desire holds him to things which his better self despises — the reign, slavery, of sin. Compare the sensual Augustine's prayer "Lord save me — but not yet!"

B. Earlier (chs. 1-3) Paul reviewed the state of Roman and Jewish society — domestically, socially, intellectually, religiously. There were division, darkness, sensuality, homosexuality, violence, dishonesty, slander, self-excuse, and mutual accusation. Religion was helpless to save society from the innate detructive forces of evil, from *the social burden* of sin.

C. A generation ago this language — *bondage, burden, etc.* — was scoffed at. Now every social survey, psychiatric clinic, public discussion of crime, every legal defense of violence, sexual assault, and murder on the grounds of "diminished responsibility" illustrates:

1. that tolerated evil blunts the conscience, darkens the mind, undermines responsibility, rots the soul and rots society;

2. that the memory of evil shadows the life, twists the judgment, sours the emotions, saps the will;

3. that the self-absorption of sin turns the soul in upon itself, against society; every wrongdoer is a social liability.

D. We talk of fear-complex, guilt-complex, power of repressed desire, anxiety, neurosis, disintegration of personality, pathological introversion, the death-wish. Paul talked of *inner bondage* and *social burden* of sin — meaning what we mean!

E. But he talked, too, of liberation -- *bondage broken, burden lifted.* The emancipation that is forgiveness and deliverance — of Christ's power to break the vicious circular chain and set men free, by the rule of His Spirit (Romans 8:2) and the forgiveness that breaks the entail of guilt and fear. That is where salvation begins.

II. Salvation provokes a spontaneous reaction — commitment: "You have become slaves of God."

A. Human nature cannot stand total freedom. Man is never at his best until overmastering purpose possesses, towering ideal drives, commanding love enslaves to great achievement. Compulsion is an element in every great character. Until we become so possessed, directed, and driven, we fulfill humdrum routines, instead of living; we drift, waste, dissipate time, at the mercy of mood, impulse, persuasion, weather, senses. Our lives are of little consequence until compelling purpose and unifying aim give direction, consistency, value, and energy to existence. The bigger the cause, the bigger we become as people. And the biggest people of all are "the servants to God."

B. Paul mentions *soldiers* with "weapons" dedicated to the war of righteousness (v. 13); *workers* for righteousness (v. 18); *colleagues* of Jesus (v. 8). In each light, commitment is complete, and we *exchange* masters (vv. 16, 17). Life is first liberated, then freely surrendered; emancipated, then dedicated. But whereas the former bondage was bitter, destructive, obsessive, and helpless, this service of righteousness and of God is healthful, joyous, free, exhilarating, ennobling. For its motivating forces are not guilt, fear, passion, and lust, but gratitude, faith, union with Christ in resurrection life (vv. 4, 5), and grace (v. 14). The free response of liberated hearts is grateful, loving service of the Liberator — else were our freedom shameful!

That free commitment to the cause of God — that, too, is salvation.

III. Salvation produces a half-conscious by-product — saintliness: "the return you get is sanctification."

A. From liberation and dedication emerges a personal goodness of unique quality and type — the Christian not only committed to good works and good warfare, but himself remade in spirit and love of goodness — clean because cleansed, straight because straightened out, loving because loved, truthful as one in whom divine truth works, Christlike because Christ's. All common integrity, morality, honesty, and healthy-mindedness is assumed. *This* is "goodness-plus."

B. Plus *gratitude, peace, joy,* radiance, and *humility,* never claiming to be good but ever striving to be better — deriving from God, aspiring to God, genuine through and through because lived out before God. Hence a certain "sacredness" of life, of others, of duty, of oneself, lies at heart of it. It is wholly God's and therefore holy. Far from sanctimonious, it is genuinely sanctified.

C. Yet it is a half-conscious *by*-product. Paul's word is "fruit" — of light within the mind (Ephesians 5:9), found in all that is good and right and true; "fruit" of the Spirit within the soul — love, joy, peace, longsuffering, gentleness, goodness, meekness, fidelity, and self-discipline. None of it *worked at,* deliberately, consciously, artificially, self-righteously: but *worked out,* as experience of the love of God and the grace of Christ refines life from within.

D. Saintliness is produced as naturally as the fragrance in a flower, the bloom on a peach, the glow on the face of a child: this, too, is salvation.

IV. Salvation involves a revised perspective — eternity: "its end, eternal life."

A. Inevitably new horizons emerge in a life so related to God. We are not liberated to be lost, nor dedicated to be cast away at last, nor sanctified to go out in darkness! All God's dealing with us in Christ, all His love, redemption, and purpose in our lives, implies immortality. "He is not God of the dead but of the living — all live to Him" (Luke 20:38).

B. Yet "eternal life" is not the Gospel's answer to only *death,* but to all limitation, frustration, perplexity, and despair that death introduces into life. Now, already, we taste immortal hope, *now* we have eternal life (John 5:24; I John 5:12) — the life originating in eternal love, mediated through eternal Christ, nourished on eternal truth, rooted among eternal things, enriched by eternal values, dedicated to eternal right, refined by eternal grace, walking already in eternal Company. That, too, is salvation.

Putting Paul's great sentence together again: Salvation is *life* — liberated, dedicated, consecrated, endless. Such life is the *gift* of God (v. 23). We *earn* our bondage, burden, and death the hard way, but are presented with *life* — if we obey from the heart the standard of teaching (v. 17) which the gospel presents to faith. As Paul said at Philippi to an enquirer, "Believe in the Lord Jesus, and you will be saved. . . ."

26. *Things that Accompany Salvation*

"Though we speak thus, yet in your case, beloved, we feel sure of better things that belong to salvation" —Hebrews 6:9

Introduction

A. The trouble with solemn warnings is that they frequently upset most those least in need of them. Earnest, conscientious people search their hearts yet more diligently and painfully, while the careless remain unmoved. Hebrews 6:1-8 is among the most solemn in scripture. It rehearses the great privileges the readers had enjoyed, sets apostasy in the worst possible light, seems to hold out no hope of second repentance, and ends with words like "worthless," "cursed," "burned."

B. Yet the writer is aware of those likely to be hurt by such bluntness; he does not believe the readers have reached such a condition, though they may be wavering and shaken. He is persuaded that the outward signs accompanying (belonging to, giving evidence of) salvation are seen in their lives. The author is not defining now what *constitutes* salvation — this is largely hidden, unprovable, known only to the inmost heart — but recalling what *manifests* a genuine salvation-experience to the individual himself and to those who observe. Much in the letter is concerned with *signs that accompany salvation.*

I. Gift of Assurance

A. Words like "confidence," "assurance," and "comfort" occur nine times in this letter. Much of the argument is designed to support assurance: the Gospel is surely attested (1:1; 2:1-4); Jesus is greater than angels (1:5-14) or Moses (3:2-6); we have a merciful Priest (4:14-16); and God has given His *promise, oath,* and *anchor* to strengthen certainty (6:13-20). So we draw near with confidence to the throne of Grace, enter with confidence the new and living way. We must not throw away our confidence but preserve it within our hearts.

B. The basis of assurance here is the faithfulness of God (6:17, 18) expressed in Christ and the Word. In Paul, the basis of assurance is the Spirit's witness to the believer's heart (Romans 8:16) — Spirit of adoption. In John, the basis is the free love of God ("now are we sons . . ." I John 3:1) and the greatness of God's heart ("if our heart condemn us, God is greater . . ." — I John 3:20). The basis is never merely in ourselves, in feelings, but in God and in His word and deed for us. Yet we know, by changes in ourselves, by peace, longing, victory, and joy, that His word has come to us, that His Spirit has dealt with us.

C. This assurance is for all. We are not saved because we have it; we have it because we are saved. It is ours to live by; it *accompanies* salvation. It is all the Lord's doing — *but it has been done!*

II. Awakening of Appetite

A. Milk is for children, meat for the mature (5:12-14). Believers taste the heavenly gift (6:4). They have an appetite for *prayer* — coming to "throne of Grace" (4:16); for *God's word* — "tasted goodness of word of God" (6:5); for Christian *service* — "your work . . . the love you showed" (6:10); for *grace* — "heart strengthened by grace, not foods" (13:9). This is the unquestionable sign of God's dealing with the soul — new hunger, tastes, longings, interests: a real symptom of life.

B. But appetite needs *guarding*. It survives wherever spiritual life survives, but is jaded, weakened, blunted by some amusements, books, friendships, interests. It needs *refining* sometimes — when (as happened at Corinth) taste fastens on excitement, the spectacular, visual, sensual, and emotional, in place of the "deep things" of God and true spiritual progress. It needs *educating*, too; a capacity for teaching, prayer, experience of God, can be developed, increased — or else remain childish, stunted, craving always the elementary and familiar, never the progressive and mature (5:11-14). A steady, advancing appetite is a *sure* sign of spiritual health.

III. Longing for Association

A. Association is referred to three times: forsake not assembling together; obey your leaders, keeping watch for your souls; remember those who spoke to you the word of God (10:25; 13:7, 17). "Let brotherly love continue" (13:1); strive for peace, avoid bitterness (13:14, 15). Association had special importance in days of persecution, but is also a sign, a symptom, of a state of heart: fellowship is infinitely precious to the truly saved.

B. Strange how it happens! Christian folk appear dull, interests narrow, obscure, faults obvious, seriousness unattractive, to outsider; but when Christ comes to the heart, the Church also is transfigured — qualities, excellences, become apparent that make Christian company, conversation, and fellowship both necessary and attractive. Being one of the Christian community does not make a Christian, but being Christian makes the community imperative.

C. So, the decline of desire for Christian fellowship betrays cooling zeal for Christ, guilty conscience, dwindling faith. Forsaking of assembling together becomes a symptom of letting slip, going backwards. Build-up of resentments, haboring of grudges, and tolerating of coldness reveal a heart whose salvation is clouded, whose Lord is distant and little loved. ("Invisible Church" is no sincere answer to this; it is not clearly a scriptural truth and offers inadequate fellowship to nourish and discipline the soul.)

Love toward all the saints is a sign of life and salvation. "Out of fellowship" usually means "out of grace."

IV. Tenacity of Adherence

A. Throughout the epistle, the clearest emphasis of all falls upon *faith* — not as trust, merely, but as steadfast fidelity to what has been known, heard, seen, and experienced of God. It is a quality of faith:

1. *That holds fast* — to profession (4:14), to confidence and pride in our hope (3:6), to confidence firm to the end (3:14), to confession of hope without wavering (10:23), to hope as an anchor (6:18);

2. *That is patient, enduring* — seven times emphasized (6:12, 15; 10:36; 11:27, 32-40; 12:1, 7);

3. *That persists* — the constant warnings — against drifting away (2:1), neglecting salvation (2:3), falling away from God (3:12), failing (4:1), falling by disobedience (4:11), sinning deliberately, spurning the Son of God (10:26, 29), throwing away confidence (10:35), shrinking back (10:39), growing weary, faint-hearted (12:3), failing to obtain grace (12:15), and refusing Him who speaks (12: 25) — indicate the quality of faith exhorted and the dangers besetting the readers.

B. Unexpected catastrophe falling upon the Jewish nation (A.D. 67-70, the final revolt and fall of Jerusalem) and the rise of intense persecution of both Jews and Christians, with the disillusion and bewilderment occasioned, probably explain the need for these warnings. The writer is persuaded that they will prove durable — endurance, tenacity, perseverance, and "spiritual obstinacy" being sure accompaniments of true salvation. Jesus Himself had said; "He who endures . . . will be saved" (Mark 13:13).

C. Yet salvation comes not without struggle, pain, despondency. Throughout the epistle, sympathy, encouragement, understanding, reminders of Christ's suffering, His temptation, tears, and intercession, reminders of heroes of faith — all show the intensity of their suffering. The sign accompanying salvation is *not* an unflinching, invulnerable armor, never dented or scratched —a soul unmoved, unhurt, untroubled by doubt: this is admirable and enjoyable, but rare! The signs are tenacity, stubbornness, perseverance, and toughness, that are often down but rise again, often hurt but fight on, frequently in conflict but refusing to be separated from the love of God in Christ.

That stubborn adherence, despite struggle, is a sure accompaniment of salvation.

V. Kindling of Aspiration

A. Because of the emphasis on "holding fast," it is important to note also the race to be run (12:1-3), the need to move on from childhood to maturity, learning to teaching (5:12-14), to seize the hope set before us (6:18), to leave elementals and go on to maturity (6:1). The restless pioneers and pilgrims of faith press towards the eternal city and unseen goal (ch. 11). This too accompanies salvation — a pressing toward the mark, a spiritual restlessness that marks a soul on pilgrimage — all the way, questing, searching, striving. "Here we have no lasting city. . . . we seek one . . ." (13:14).

B. This is the paradox of the saved soul: it has assurance, yet still strives toward maturity, completeness; has tasted, yet still hungers for greater satisfaction; enjoys fellowship, but longs to broaden its circle; is tenacious and steadfast, yet presses to new forward positions. Striving is not salvation — you are not saved because you strive, but strive because you *are* saved. The heart conscious of this kindled, unsatisfied aspiration may be sure God is dealing with it in grace.

Once more — because it is important: assurance, appetite, association, adherence, aspiration *do not constitute salvation*. Deliverance from sin, through personal faith in Christ alone, *defines* salvation. But these things *accompany* the experience, as evidence and signs that grace is working within our hearts.

27. Attitude — Art — Adventure

"Make love your aim" — I Corinthians 14:1

Introduction

A. A pity, here, to paraphrase Paul. He says "pursue," "press after" love. At Luke 17:23, the word is translated "follow"; it means in fact intensive, energetic, purposeful "going after" something, someone, whether with good or bad intent.

B. Paul is thus transcribing into bare ethical terms Christ's "Follow Me." The Gospel invitation involves certainly more than ethics —

faith in His leading, imitation, and identification with Him. But in the simplest *practical* terms all Christian behavior and relationships are deducible from "follow after love."

C. Jesus Himself declared love the crown of God's law — the culmination and concentration of all the commandments (Matthew 22:35-40). Paul taught that love fulfilled all obligations (Romans 13:8-10). John held that in love we behold the nature of God and the essence of Christianity (I John 4:7, 8, 16). The second epistle of Peter sees love as the crown of all Christian character-development (II Peter 1:5-7).

D. Ignorance, therefore, of the meaning of love is ignorance of everything. Yet who can define it?

I. Recalling such incidents, stories, examples, as enshrine the many-sidedness of love, one thinks of:

A. Damien, ministering singlehanded to 600 lepers at Molokai; redeeming an appalling situation by tenacity, devotion, and toil, until struck down himself — *love's selflessness*.

B. The Quaker leader, refusing to abandon a New England village settlement and seek shelter in forests from advancing Indians; remaining, unarmed, with unlocked door and welcoming latchet hanging outside; quietly going to prayer and sleep; hearing an Indian approach and place a white feather of peace in thatch above the door — *love's pacificism*.

C. Livingstone's home at Blantyre, Scotland, filled with records, relics, possessions — including his *sword!* For he accepted the Queen's commission and pursued with purposeful sword slave-raiders who kidnapped the Africans he loved — *love's realism and strength*.

D. John Inglesant, courtier of 17th-century England, who, having found his brother Eustace stabbed by an Italian conspirator Malvolti, vowed undying revenge, pursued to and throughout Italy, brooding always on vengeance: finding the assassin, denouncing him as a criminal and cut-throat — yet at plea for mercy, taking him to the village Church; and after prayer and sacrament, refusing to put Malvolti to death, handing him over to the Church and the "vengeance of God." (Years later in Naples, Inglesant found one man ceaselessly ministering amidst plague, followed him to the hovel of a leper to see him die exhausted — Malvolti, now a devoted grey friar) — *love's restraint* upon passion.

E. "Abbe Pierre," in post-war France, strenuously campaigning for rehousing poorest, raising millions of francs by unorthodox, relentless exposures and publicity — publicly inviting the Minister of Reconstruction to the funeral of 3-year-old frozen to death; televising the story of an eviction-order found in hand of woman dead on the pavement; stirring the conscience of Church and State by protest and action — "that there might be a little less suffering in the world, and God a little less misunderstood" — *love's ruthlessness*.

F. Jesus and Peter in John 21; as, deliberately, the erring disciple is made to recall his bold boast, to retrace his threefold denial with a threefold confession of love, warned of tests still to come, bidden to start again: "Follow Me"; there is no easier way to make Christian men — *love's sternness*.

G. Jesus in the house of Simon the Pharisee, publicly exposing churlish inhospitality by comparing it with the loving attentions given him by woman of the city — and leading Simon into admission that little love means little forgiveness: an amazing scene of ruthless exposure of self-righteous snobbery! (Luke 7:36f.) — *love's anger*.

Love is plainly many-sided, flexible, varying yet consistent in expression, calculating the consequences for others, never for itself: basically, a steadfast, shrewd, persistent, undiscourageable *attitude* of good will; it is *the* Christian secret of character, the cement for new society, the answer to all problems of relationship, the law of heaven for life on earth.

II. Christian love is a firm principle, not an emotion: yet "attitude," alone, is too hard a word:

A. Memory recalls one who in three years never did obvious kindness in an obvious way — transporting a poor lad's cheap, battered typewriter, added typing-paper as a gracious surprise; giving a lonely old soul a much-needed monetary-gift, wrapped in a box of home-made sweetmeats; taking an injured schoolchild-stranger to the hospital, "finding" a child's magazine in his pocket; "happening along" when a frightened patient was due to hear his delayed diagnosis-report. Another person, every Friday evening, for 18 years, reading to a blind man, never *once* asking for postponement. Another, a prominent and influential lady respected by all, walking the length of High Street on a busy shopping morning, chatting to an unmarried mother on first appearance with her baby. . . .

B. Love is resourceful, sensitive, shrewd, and secretive; rejecting the obvious, ill-considered impulse, it finds the artful method. It is perfect in timing, retentive of names, troubles, stories, always aware when silence is kindness. When speaking, it fits words to wounds — *never* forgetting how "kindness" can hurt, how interest can become interference, how remembered assistance and confidences can ruin friendship.

C. "Love is courteous" (I Corinthians 13:4-7), anticipating ever the hidden feelings of others. Jesus takes the blind man aside privately lest his excited gesticulations at returning sight amuse the crowd (Mark 8:22-25); He patiently engages the deaf and dumb in pantomime of signs — again in private — to establish communication (Mark 7:32-35); He enters calming conversation with the insane (Mark 5:1-13); He so manages to raise the daughter of Jairus that neither she nor the village know if she were dead (Mark 5:35-43); He not only heals but *touches* the leper (Mark 1:40-42).

D. For this wit, cleverness, imagination, swift insight, and self-trans-portation into others' shoes, the only fitting word is "art." Love *is* an attitude, but has learned an *art* — else it is prone to be clumsy, blundering, and blind.

III. Yet love has abundant reward. We *see* people, individuals, characters, often as never before; with new interest, transfigured. We walk abroad in a world of friends, or potential friends, instead of rivals, foes. *We* are enlarged in understanding, sympathy, and experience.

A. Tolstoi: "The powerful means of achieving true happiness in life is . . . to spread out from oneself, in every direction, like a spider, a whole spider's web of love and to catch in it everything that comes along — whether an old woman or a child, a girl or a policeman."

B. R. Law: "Love is the power to live not only for another but in another, to realize one's own fullest life in the fulfilment of other lives. . . . If I love my neighbour as myself, I regale myself with his prosperity, even as I share the bitter cup of his adversity; I am honoured in his praise, promoted in his advancement, gladdened in his joy, even as I am humbled in his shame or distressed in his sin."

C. Thus all *my* experience is enriched, elaborated, exalted, by the outgoing of soul that is *love*:

> *O doom beyond the saddest guess,*
> *As the long years of God unroll,*
> *To make thy dreary selfishness*
> *The prison of a soul!*

Christian love is a firm, realistic *attitude;* a shrewd, imaginative *art;* an endless exploration and *adventure.*
Follow after love.

28. *What Price Freedom?*

"Live as free men, yet without using your freedom as a pretext for evil; but live as servants of God." —I Peter 2:16

Introduction

Surely this is a fitting text for Independence Day, since for individuals and nations independence and freedom are inseparable experiences — or two sides of the same precious coin. And with splendid economy and insight, Peter compresses into one exhortation the *privilege*, the *peril*, and the *perfection* of freedom.

I. Freedom is a privilege — the privilege of the mature.

A. It is not an automatic or a natural right. The claim, "all men are born free" is nonsense. From the child's first days all kinds of rules, safeguards, and civilizing patterns of behavior discipline him without his consent or understanding. Social pressures of education, character-training, group loyalty, and family unity close in upon the growing lad, providing security and stimulating growth, but also restraining antisocial impulses. Soon he travels the same route each day, at the same times, to attend to the set lessons — because society says he should. He must wash his neck, keep decently clothed, clean his teeth, practice accepted rules of hygiene. In scores of ways, patterns derived from past experience and accepted by the majority mold the individual new life, demanding responses of appreciation and obedience. So all men are born under authority: they have to *achieve* freedom, as a privilege.

B. The immature are so disciplined because they do not understand the conditions of their own welfare. With development, truth begins to make them free, because it confers understanding, and with understanding comes free and willing acceptance of life's necessary conditions, the appreciation of good for its own sake, and ready co-operation with it. These are all marks of moral adulthood, of maturity of mind, achieving its freedom.

C. So Peter argues: the spiritually mature manage to live well without the compulsion of law: they are "free men." They remain subject to legal institutions (honoring emperors, governors, etc.) but they "do right," and "maintain good conduct," because they see it is right, and for the sake of Christian witness, and not from compulsion or through fear: they *willingly* obey — as free men.

79

D. So Paul argues, too: the spiritually mature live well *high above the law*, bringing forth fruits of the Spirit in a realm of virtue where commandment and obligation are not the main motive ("about such there is no law").

It is on this level of spiritual autonomy, of freedom achieved by maturity, that the Christian is exhorted to live: high privilege indeed!

II. Freedom is, nevertheless, a peril too.

A. It is so, certainly, for the undisciplined individual. Physically, psychologically, and morally we are creatures of habit, fastening our own chains upon ourselves even while we protest our liberty. Whosoever sets out "to do what the devil he likes" will inevitably end doing what the devil likes — long after he himself has ceased to like it.

B. It is so, no less, for society. Most vicious things spawn under the cloak of freedom — as Peter here suggests. Every rebellion against established standards raises the banner of someone's "liberties": pornography flourishes in the name of publishers' freedom to follow art for art's sake — provided it pays; filth, falsehood, slander are defended as "freedom of the press"; gambling halls multiply in the name of freedom, so that a few may exploit the weakness and avarice of others; freedom to persuade others to drink is preserved so that enormous fortunes are won by trading with tragedy, alcoholism, and accident. No one believes these crusaders for public liberty, but the hypocritical propaganda serves its malign purpose: such "freedom" is destructive.

C. Even to the Christian, the assertion of freedom can be specious. Spiritual freedom is not liberty of personal inclination. Some once contended that the "spiritually free" are exempt from taxation (see Matthew 17:24f.)! Others felt able to defy the law, and teach men so (Matthew 5:19). Yet others contended morality did not apply under grace (Romans 6:1). One may still sometimes hear the argument that "man-made laws" (concerning train tickets, motoring, customs duties) may be evaded without shame. It is the oldest of all heresies, and the serpent's original philosophy, that obedience has no place in paradise. Law and prophets, epistles and gospels, conscience and Christ, all flatly deny it. The Christian is bound to the obedience of faith.

No one is ever above the temptation to do what he likes and miscall it spiritual freedom . . . to his eternal peril.

III. For the perfection of freedom is bondage to God.

A. "As servants of God" live as free men — though one may also read "slaves." Religion, by ancient definition, is that which "binds" — man's only ennobling bondage. Peter means that, above the inevitable pressures of society and the higher self-rule of mature moral understanding, life is subject to the will of God, because its welfare also is rooted in that will.

B. Peter has much to say of life so rooted in God's will:

Christians live no longer by human passions but by the will of God (4:2)

It is God's will that by right-doing we put to silence the ignorance of foolish men (2:15)

It is better to suffer for doing right than for doing wrong, if such be God's will (as it might be — 3:17)

Let those who suffer according to God's will commit the keeping of their souls to Him . . . (4:19)

Life rooted in God's will is not easy, then, but it is strong and safe.

C. Thus, for Peter, Christians are "elect unto obedience," "children of obedience," "purified in obedience," and have "sanctified Christ in their hearts as *Lord*." The emphasis is unmistakable. As his readers struggle with the implications of faith amid the multifarious compulsions of the Roman world, Peter would have them remember those *inner* compulsions, in obedience to which lies highest freedom.

Conclusion

All the very great. live under such liberating compulsions. Even Jesus said, "I must," not once but *nine* recorded times. The soul attains its Independence Day when it asserts its freedom from the bondage of society, sin, and self, and its bondage to the compulsion of the highest —

> *Make me a captive, Lord,*
> *And then I shall be free:*
> *Force me to render up my sword*
> *And I shall conqueror be.*
> *I sink in life's alarms*
> *When by myself I stand:*
> Imprison me *within Thine arms*
> *And strong shall be my hand.*

29. *Paul's Asides*

"To whom I belong and whom I worship . . . Who strengthens me . . . Who loved me and gave himself for me." —Acts 27:23; Philippians 4:13; Galatians 2:20

Introduction

However carefully we frame our words — sometimes to hide our thoughts — it is our accent, our asides, our unpremeditated afterthoughts, that often give us away. A rich mind, especially, will overflow in half-intentional expressions that suggest thought on thought and reveal a full heart. So Paul, in the heat of inspiration, throws in phrase after phrase striving to share all he sees; and even then, at the beloved name of God or of Christ, will add an afterthought in which we feel the strong pulse of his faith and love, beating almost unconsciously. Here are three such self-revealing afterthoughts.

I. "To whom I belong, and whom I worship."

A. This is a simple statement of fact, a declaration of allegiance, and of the confidence in God's care that arises therefrom. It implies no self-righteous claim to special divine favor or to exceptional devotion: it defines where Paul stands.

B. The issue in mind is the personal safety of Paul, of his Roman escort, the ship's crew, and other passengers, on this storm-tossed grain ship making for Rome late in the year and faced now for days with imminent danger of wreck. Sailors resort to superstitious vows, soldiers to their curses; Paul remains the coolest on board.

"Sirs, I exhort you to be of good cheer" — faith is a fundamentally cheerful frame of mind;

"There shall be no loss of any man's life among you" — the trusting heart often foresees how things will turn out;

"There stood by me . . . an angel of God to whom I belong, saying, Fear not. . . ." — there lies his confidence: he belongs to God, is God's servant, *God's responsibility*.

C. So the little man with the large heart outmatched sailors in courage and Romans in stoicism. The servant of the Most High need not worry about his personal welfare. All the matters about which he is uncertain are in safe hands.

D. Yet this is no fanatical, unreasoning assurance of final safety. The whole purpose of that journey to Rome was that he might stand trial for his life. Deliverance from the sea meant deliverance into Caesar's hands! The future remains menacing. What Paul knows, *with such conviction that it slips into speech casually,* is that he can leave the uncertain future with God, be of good cheer, and face the immediate day with good appetite — "Wherefore . . . I pray you take some meat."

E. Months before, confronted with warnings of imprisonment, the same deep confidence and practical common sense in facing one day at a time underlay Paul's answer, "None of these things move me. . . ." Months later, awaiting Caesar's sentence, the same sublime trust writes, "For me to live is Christ, to die is gain. To live in the flesh means added service; to die is to be with Christ, which is far better. Which I shall choose I know not. . . ."

This is the only confidence in which God's work can be truly and freely done: unafraid of men, of failure, of the future, knowing that while you care for God's service He careth for you.

II. "Who strengthens me."

A. This unexpected phrase is added to Paul's note of thanks to the Philippians for gifts sent during his imprisonment. Their generosity prompted a long look backward over his varied life and changing fortunes. He began as a wealthy Jew and Pharisee: now he is glad to accept gifts from Gentiles. There have been times, he writes, when I had plenty; other times of great want. Sometimes I have been well fed, at other times actually hungry. Again (a third contrast) there have been times when I was able to walk among proud men conscious of possessing equal resources; at other times in such company I have been "humbled" (as only poor men can feel humbled) (see Philippians 4:12, 13). Such variation of circumstance marked his whole career.

B. Philippi provides a perfect illustration of such fluctuation. There Paul stays first in the hospitable home of wealthy Lydia, in luxury. Then suddenly he is thrown, bleeding and hungry, into jail. Just as suddenly, he finds himself sitting at supper in the jailer's residence, attended by official servants, heaped with plenty. In the morning, the city leaders apologize to him!

C. In all such vicissitudes, Paul does not lose heart or head. On the one hand, "I am instructed, initiated into the secret, of having and not having" — *having*, without gluttony, pride, selfishness, or worldliness; or *not having*, without envy, resentment, or covetousness. This is a spiritual wisdom about wealth and poverty that only those instructed by God and experience can ever learn.

D. On the other hand, Paul says, "I am content, self-sufficient — I can manage without — *for Christ enables me*." Earlier, he has exhorted the Philippians to let their evenness, their "being always the same," be noticeable to all, and he has offered as the secret of such equanimity the assurance that in all circumstances "the Lord is near." Here, by a seemingly chance phrase he reveals that this is precisely his own secret: "I can endure, put up with, all things, through Him who is at hand to strengthen me."

This is the only faith in which God's work can be steadfastly done — the conviction that every want will be supplied, for workers and work, and that every varying circumstance can be cheerfully borne through Him who constantly strengthens us.

III. "Who loved me and gave himself for me."

A. Once more the additional phrase, at the end of a thought, takes us right into the secret chambers of Paul's soul. He has been recalling (Galatians 1 and 2) the salient points of his spiritual career — his heart-breaking disappointment with Judaism, his struggles, his attempts to shake off doubt by violence against the Church; then the sudden revelation of the Son of God, the years of rethinking in Arabia, the first Christian work attempted in Tarsus and Antioch, and the first fellowship with the mother-Church in Jerusalem. All this he reveiws and summarizes as "the life which I now live" — an apostle, evangelist, writer, warrior.

B. How changed it all is! New hopes, faith, techniques, interests, fellowships, aims, experiences crowd his life now. But all is due to *faith* in the Son of God. Yet that was not the beginning: behind Paul's faith and surrender and decision lay God's prior revelation of Jesus to him; behind that, God's choice of Paul "from my mother's womb"; behind even that, Christ's giving of Himself for Paul; and behind all, the original and ultimate source of all Paul's new life, "He loved me."

C. That is the unchanging center of Paul's changeful story, the deepest motive-force of his far-ranging career. This, he means to say, made me what I am, makes me do the things I do, sustains me through every threatening circumstance, drives me forward: "He loved me, and gave himself for me." Too easily and too often, with us, other motives for service intrude: some love of self-expression, pride of place, desire for popularity, wistful hope of purchasing ease of conscience, desire to lead or to dominate, or sense of intellectual or spiritual superiority. Soon we forget where we began, and come to talk much about our work, what we have done for Him, our love, and our giving of ourselves. Paul's talk is only of His love, and His giving of Himself for Paul. The greatest of all Christ's workers reiterates his secret: *"He* loved *me"*; and the profoundest of all Christian thinkers echoes the truth — "We love . . . because He first loved us."

This is the only motive that will sustain us in God's work with unwearying persistence, unflagging zeal, undiminished joy, and a perpetually humble spirit.

Conclusion

Such is the threefold foundation of all true Christian service: the overriding confidence that leaves all uncertainties, consequences, and results in God's hands; the undergirding strength that faces all vicissitudes, wants, and adversities in the strength of Christ; the inexhaustible inspiration and selfless gratitude that suffices for every challenge and every situation — "To whom I belong . . . Who strengthens me . . . Who loved me."

30. *The Divine Voice*

A voice came from heaven . . . the crowd standing by heard it and said
that it had thundered. Others said, "An angel has spoken to him." Jesus
answered, "This voice has come for your sake. . . ." —John 12:28-30

Introduction

1. In one swift sentence, three levels of spiritual discernment are represented. All are agreed that there is a sound, a noise. To the crowd it
seems a meaningless rumble, with a natural, commonplace explanation.
A few, sensing the tension of the moment and the weight of Christ's
words, are aware of some vaguely divine meaning — "an angel spoke."
To Jesus, it was a clear message from the Father. One event, three
reactions—

> *the crowd, spiritually unresponsive, explain it away;*
> *the few, spiritually impressionable, dimly discerning, are awed;*
> *the One, spiritually attuned, hears a divine word.*

2. Jesus often emphasized this difference in the spiritual capacity of
people, contrasting the wise and prudent with "babes" (the unsophisti-
cated), and Pharisees and scribes with publicans and harlots. The parable of the sower is on this theme; and the warning "He that hath ears
to hear, let him hear" lends it solemnity. For this varying capacity to
read the spiritual meaning of things affects all our understanding — of
the world, of history, and of experience.

I. Of the world

A. To some observers, the material world presents only a confused
mass of unintelligible facts, which conflicting scientific theories only
make more puzzling. It seems a vast universe, strange, bewildering,
menacing, meaningless, whose distances baffle imagination, whose
forces frighten, whose origin and destiny are unknown. To such the
hurrying, teeming world is incomprehensible: it merely "thunders."

B. To others, the whole created world appears a procession of order
and beauty; of things to laugh at, sing about, thrill to; of things to
lift the heart above nature. For them, purpose and hope gleam through
a multitude of facts; philosophers, scientists, musicians, and poets
discern —

> *a sense sublime*
> *Of something far more deeply interfused,*
> *Whose dwelling is the light of setting suns,*
> *And the round ocean and the living air,*
> *And the blue sky, and in the mind of man;*
> *A motion and a spirit, that impels*
> *All thinking things, all objects of all thought,*
> *And rolls through all things.*

C. But to those who learn of Jesus, "the heavens declare the glory of God and the firmament showeth his handiwork"; —

> *Nature is but a name for an effect*
> *Whose cause is God* — (Cowper)

for in sun, rain, face of sky, or child, lilies, grass, fowls of the air, wayward wind, bread, fish, seedtime, harvest — Jesus taught that "Nature is the glass reflecting God" (Young). Listening with Jesus to the pulse of life through all that moves, breathes, lives and loves, the Christian hears neither thunder nor angels, but the heavenly Father —

> *His are the mountains and the valleys His,*
> *And the resplendent rivers. His to enjoy*
> *With a propriety that none can feel,*
> *But who, with filial countenance inspired,*
> *Can lift to heaven an unpresumptuous eye,*
> *And smiling say — My Father made them all!*

> (Cowper)

The facts being given, adequate interpretation depends on spiritual perception: Hebrews 11:3.

II. Of history

A. To some history is only the ceaseless march of conquering feet; the record of man's repeated follies, endless tragedy leading nowhere — "that great dust-heap called 'history'" (Birrell) — "only a confused heap of facts" (Chesterfield) — "the record of a man in quest of his daily bread and butter" (van Loon) — "a distillation of rumour" (Carlyle) — "little more than the register of the crimes, follies and misfortunes of mankind" (Gibbon).

B. To others, "the historian is a prophet looking backwards": not all is tragedy, folly, sin; *something* gleams as supernatural behind it — fate, destiny, stars, providence, "angels." "The use of history is to give value to the present hour and its duty" (Emerson) — reading lessons of experience, heroism, courage, warning, morality. "The world's history is the world's judgement" (Schiller).

C. But to those who learn of Jesus, the history of man is summarized in "My Father worketh hitherto. . . ." The Bible becomes the record of history's meaning, and the foresight of its goal — as the age-long experience of men and nations becomes the vehicle of divine self-revelation. "History is God's patient explanation to man of eternal principles" (Beard). All history is preparation for Christ, and exposition of Christ, leading to consummation in Christ.

The events being given, adequate understanding depends on spiritual insight: Luke 12:56.

III. Of experience

A. To some, it is mere "thunder," concatenation of accidents, injustices, ill luck, mistakes, good fortune, inheritance, health, mystery; a strange medley of contradictions — of sunlight, shade, duty, delight, shocks, surprises, dreams, and disillusion; barely controllable, wholly unpredictable, mainly disappointing, always capricious. "Experience — a poor little hut constructed from the ruins of the palace of gold and marble called our illusions" (Roux). Its message — luck and pride, or heartbreak, madness, despair.

B. To others, experience is "the mother of knowledge" (Breton), — "an arch, to build upon" (Adams),

> *"an arch wherethro'*
> *Gleams that untravelled world whose margin fades*
> *For ever and for ever when I move."*
>
> (Tennyson)

Philosophers, moralists, educationists read the riddle of man's daily circumstance to find wisdom, profit, progress: seers and poets sometimes discern mercy and goodness at the heart of things —

> . . . there suddenly broke in on him like a sunrise a sense of God's mercy — Out of the cruel North most of the birds had flown south from ancient instinct, and would return to keep the wheel of life moving. Merciful! But some remained, snatching safety by cunning ways from the winter of death. Merciful! Under the fetters of ice and snow there were little animals lying snug in holes, and fish under the frozen streams, and bears asleep in their lie-ups, and moose stamping out their yards, and caribou rooting for their grey moss. Merciful! And human beings, men, women, and children, fending off winter and sustaining life by an instinct old as that of the migrating birds: one man nursing like a child another whom he had known less than a week. . . . Surely, surely, behind the reign of law and the coercion of power there was a deep purpose — of mercy (Buchan).

Such faintly catch in human experience the echo of the whisper of an angel's voice —

> *a divinity that shapes our ends,*
> *Rough-hew them how we will.*

C. But to those who learn of Jesus, experience is the felt faithfulness of a loving Father, who knows, cares, guides, hears prayer, meets need, gives good things, saves sinners, welcomes to everlasting life. To Christian hearts, *all* things — tribulation, distress, persecution, famine, nakedness, peril, sword, death, life, things present or to come — work, work together, and work for good. For we are His children, and our days at His disposing, our experience shaped by His hand, for His gracious purpose. *The elements of daily life being given,* adequate spiritual reaction depends on knowing God (Romans 8:28).

Conclusion

So outside Damascus, some heard only noise, but Paul heard the voice that transformed the world, history, and experience by transforming himself. We need pray constantly, "Speak, Lord, for Thy servant *heareth.*"

31. *Shouldn't We Begin at Jerusalem?*

A Missionary Sermon

"Repentance and forgiveness of sins should be preached in his name to all nations, beginning from Jerusalem." —Luke 24:47

Introduction

1. "Beginning from Jerusalem" — odd text for a missionary sermon, but surely right. Motives and arguments for missionary enterprise are various: compassion, obedience, persecution, spiritual investment in dark days. There is another, rarely pleaded but valid, perhaps to some minds more appealing — a kind of unselfish, spiritual *self-interest.*

2. Every time we talk missions someone is sure to urge needs at home: "our own land the real mission-field"; "the clamoring opportunities in our materialist urban life"; "nearer obligations of our neo-pagan culture." Jerusalem — *our Jerusalem* — must have priority! Good enough. By all means listen to the Master, begin at Jerusalem. We shall rapidly discover, though, that we cannot do our work at Jerusalem if we stay only there: we shall find that we cannot be truly Christian at Jerusalem if the ends of the earth are not in our hearts and prayers; the Church at home cannot *be* the Church unless her frontiers, horizons, representatives are abroad.

3. Under the laws of the Kingdom, missions prove for the Church at home a profitable business, and the missionary vision a sanctified self-interest. This was William Carey's contention, and has been the

modern Church's wondering discovery; experience has justified it *four-fold.*

I. Quickening

A. Pearce Carey has a telling description of the time into which William Carey came with his revolutionary challenge to world evangelism — "that century of reaction, when the mercury fell low, when reason clipped faith's wings, enthusiasm was a reproach, religion 'icily regular'; critics held the field, Hume was the oracle; Voltaire, 'that Philistine of transcendent cleverness,' the idol; Gibbon was subjecting the warm wonder of first Christian centuries to cool analysis, and 'all people of discernment had discovered Christianity to be factitious.' " In such a time, Carey felt the lifelessness of the Church . . . "knew the sparse worshippers, the coarse choristers, the neglected parishes, the Sabbath drink-revels. In Nonconformity he was familiar with spent enthusiasms, barren and bitter disputations, littleness and lowness of ideal and of life. He had only to recall how decayed he had found the Baptist cause at Moulton, how weak and strife-torn the Meeting in Earls Barton, and how disgraced Harvey Lane with its drinking pastor and deacons . . . 'College Lane's dissension and distress.' Oakham's 'feebleness,' Braunston's 'supineness,' " — all Churches he personally knew and ministered to.

B. Such was the age. Begin at Jerusalem! But Carey did just that. The first tasks to which he put his hand were to reopen, revive, "dilapidated Moulton," give support to despondent Earls Barton. Later he assumed heavy and troubled responsibility of "Harvey Lane." The preacher with the whole world in his heart gave himself without restraint to the little, lost, village causes.

C. The result? When in due course the missionary torch flared among these Churches *they* were first to feel warmth kindling in their fellowships, a new spirit of life, hope, enterprise, and prayer, awakening in their hearts. Only seven years later, Rippon could record: "More of our meeting-houses enlarged within the last five years, more built within the last fifteen, than built and enlarged for thirty years — and yet, it is necessary for many more to lengthen their cords and strengthen their stakes."

D. That echo of Carey's famous pioneering sermon is hardly accidental: The "ends of the earth" had made Jerusalem alive again; dying Churches *at home* found again their faith, zeal, power when Carey called them *abroad.*

II. Liberation

A. Job 42:10 — literally, "the Lord turned the *captivity* of Job, when he prayed for his friends" — states a Biblical principle. Freedom always comes through concern for others' bondage, not for one's own. Self-pity enslaves; absorption in others' needs liberates from our own.

B. This, too, is vividly illustrated in missionary-minded Churches, especially those out of which the modern mission movement was born. Wesley's evangelical revival had stirred England; the tide had turned and *waited to flow*. But the Established Church, and many free evangelical groups, resisted the dynamic of the Spirit — mainly because they were held in a rigid intellectual creed, imperfectly understood, which insulated hearts and Churches from the advancing evangelical fires.

C. A misunderstanding of Calvinist theology shackled evangelistic zeal. "Only the elect can be saved: and only God knows who they are!" Thought and enterprise were imprisoned, the gates of Jerusalem firmly closed . . . until Carey's explosive vision snapped shackles, burst doors, and in defiance of narrow logic and narrower loyalties the highest of High Calvinists began to give, pray, preach that heathen might be saved. The "ends of the earth" made *Jerusalem* free.

D. Some new, shattering demand of similar explosive power might well be the best tonic our homeland Churches could experience today — or the *same* demand, felt again with original intensity and force.

III. Unity

A. It is the Church's constant experience that the two factors which most powerfully unite Christians are outward persecution and the inward compulsion to reach outward in service and mission. Even the apostolic Church was divided, uncertain, ingrown in some degree (Acts 5:1-11; 6:1; 9:26; 11:1-3; 15:1-6) until the Pauline world mission drew the Church together in fellowship of effort, vision, prayer, and giving (e.g., Gentile collection for saints at Jerusalem). Deeper unity sprang from farther outreach.

B. Carey, to quote the pioneer again, had regretted "the present divided state of Christendom," looked for "the friendliest communication" of all missionary societies, and contributed immediately to *Moravian* missions, though his circle was Baptist. He strove, while faithful to convictions, "to forget the distinctions that divide." Missionary zeal always overflows boundaries of sect — all evangelical enthusiasm always does — "the light which Carey kindled spread from hill to hill like beacon fires, till every Christian Church in turn recognized the signal and responded to the call" (Greenhough).

C. Unity for its own sake is an ineffective cause: unity for some far-reaching, over-riding purpose is a far different matter. To this day it is *mission* that *unites*; the main *spiritual* pressures toward emergence of the world Church have come along missionary channels from younger Churches. Begin at Jerusalem! But to hold Jerusalem together, remember "the ends of the earth."

IV. Enrichment

A. Jerusalem — the "home" Church — may stand in urgent need, but it owes much of what it has to "the ends of the earth." Even *financially*: the missionary vision has unlocked treasuries, stimulated generosity, caused more money to flow through the Churches than any other movement in Christendom.

B. Even more is this true of *personnel*. Of the outstanding Christian leaders of the last two centuries, a high proportion were missionaries, and many more will acknowledge inspiration — and spiritual ambition — kindled by the mission cause.

C. And what access of devotion, faith, prayer, expectancy, steadfast hope has come to home Churches from an unfolding missionary story, none can measure. But it is certain that Western Christianity has been enormously enriched by whatever it has *given* to the "foreign field."

D. With world perspective in mind, the point is still more obvious. Turn the leaves of an Indian portfolio of Christian art, noting the unfamiliar symbols, fresh conceptions, imagination unfettered by tradition, and realize what a world of new insights and appreciations Eastern Churches have to offer to the sum of Christian wisdom. A curious youngster asked a retiring missionary, "What do African Christians add to the Church as a whole?" The answer, without hesitation: "Laughter, lad, laughter and song. You have never heard a Christian congregation sing until three hundred African Christians improvise a 'spiritual' in eight-part harmony!" And already, there is evidence that the younger Churches have their gifted scholars, thinkers, and propagandists.

Conclusion

Begin at Jerusalem! You soon find you only quicken, liberate, unite, and enrich Churches of the homeland when you go out, in thought and prayer, to the ends of the earth. This is "spiritual self-interest." *Whenever* you obey the Master, you do yourself a power of good!

32. Burden, Cross, and Thorn

"God is treating you as sons." —Hebrews 12:7

Introduction

1. The epistle to the Hebrews is especially perceptive in its dealing with the problems of unexpected adversity, disappointment, and danger in Christian life. The readers' traditional ideas of divine "blessing," as guaranteeing health, prosperity, and all security, may have unfitted them to face the realities of persecution (10:32), delayed hope (10:36), hostility (12:3), doubt (3:19; 4:1), deep discouragement (10:39) — and perhaps the overwhelming shock of the destruction of Jerusalem (12:25-26?). Altogether, God's dealing with them, since their conversion, perplexed, disturbed, and disappointed them.

2. The epistle's answer is, "God is treating you as sons." But the sure mark of acknowledged sonship is a father's care for discipline and education, for progress and growth. The fatherless, unwanted, often illegitimate, wild street Arabs of the ancient East were known by their untamed indiscipline to belong to no one (12:8). Though "all discipline seems at the time to be painful" (12:11), it nevertheless reveals the Father's loving responsibility, foresight, and pride in His sons. In this light, adversity is but the shade of the Father's guiding hand, and suffering may be the very badge of sonship (5:8).

3. This general explanation of God's harder dealings with us is analyzed further, in New Testament teaching, in three simple metaphors of adversity:

I. The burden

A. "Each man will have to bear his own load" (Galatians 6:5). This is the normal, inescapable effort involved in living, the duties, dangers, and demands that fall to every man. It includes the toil by which he lives, the struggle for growth and learning, the responsibility of home, family, vocation. It includes the price we pay for competing, or co-operating, with others; and our infirmities, handicaps, limitations, physical needs. The burden is universal — no life escapes unless it is a passenger, and cravenly lives on others. Full manhood requires that we shoulder our own: "sons" must accept the status and responsibilities of sonship.

B. But the Bible offers us two resources:

Faith: "Cast your burden on the Lord, and he will sustain you"

(Psalm 55:22) ; "Come unto Me . . . heavy-laden" (Matthew 11:28).
Carry the burden of life Christ's way, and we find the yoke easy, the
burden light.

Fellowship: as in a family, or friendship, or Church. "Bear ye one
another's burdens" (Galatians 6:2). Faith gives strength, and fellowship gives sympathy, for braver bearing of the appointed load.

II. The cross

A. Unlike the burden, the cross is neither universal, inescapable, nor
inseparable from living at all; but it is inseparable from *Christian*
living, and it is inescapable to disciples. "If any man come after me,
let him take up his cross. . . ." This is the vital clue to what the
cross means.

B. We have belittled "cross-bearing" to trivial annoyances — a summer
cold, someone's temper, losing things, an earache: in this way we betray
Christ's great word. The cross is *the cost of being a disciple,* whatever
inescapable hardships, loss, discipline, peril, Christianity costs us: the
anguish of self-mastery, the pain of ill-adjustment to our family, or
to the pagan world, humiliation, scorn, loneliness, material loss suffered
for conscience' sake, the agony of surrender to God's will, the discipline
of obedience to God's law. The cross is the price of following Jesus
on to the end and up to the limit.

C. For this high price of loyalty, the Bible offers us the comfort of
    sharing with all the prophets and saints in loyalty to the truth ("so
      persecuted they the prophets which were before you")
    especially of sharing the passion of Christ (we "suffer with Him.
      . . . Hereunto ye were called. . . . You shall indeed drink the
      cup that I drink of. . . .")
    reward "in heaven" ("great is your reward in heaven . . . if
    we suffer, we shall also reign with Him").
But after all, the cross we bear is His cross — that is comfort and reward enough.

III. The thorn

A. Some hardships and sufferings are neither universal nor inescapable
for Christians, but entirely personal, and quite private to individual
lives. With Paul it was "infirmity" — either of his general health, or
an affliction of his eyesight (note Galatians 4:13-15) ; it was something
painful (a "thorn"), disabling ("to buffet me"), frustrating and con-
tinuous (see II Corinthians 12:8).

B. Besides his burden and his cross, this was an added, particular trial,
which weakened his body, troubled his spirit, and harassed his prayers.
Thrice he prayed, and thrice he was refused, adding deeply to his pain.
Many lives are so afflicted, exceptionally, apparently "unfairly." All

complaint, comparison with others, and rebellion are just futile: the thorn remains.

C. But the Bible offers two assurances:

1. *Insight to understand* God's purposes, or at least to know there is a purpose. In Paul's case, it was, "Lest I be exalted above measure"; it may be very different in our case. But always there *is* a purpose — God treats us as sons. To explain it, others would have to know all the secrets of our hearts and of God's; we ourselves shall surely know, if we submit and ask. The special discipline always evidences a special purpose — or a special need.

2. *Grace to endure* God's will — "My grace is sufficient for thee," and again, "My strength is made perfect in weakness." His grace is sufficient, that is, for our endurance, and patience, and peace; and His strength is made "perfect" in that His is most clearly seen when ours is least evident.

Such insight and grace make any thorn bearable.

Conclusion

Christian life is most certainly not all burden, cross, and thorn. But when they come, always it is because God is "treating us as sons."

33. *Lord, When Did We...?*

Then the righteous will answer him, "Lord, when did we see thee hungry and feed thee, or thirsty and give thee drink? And when did we see thee a stranger and welcome thee, or naked and clothe thee? And when did we see thee sick or in prison and visit thee?" —Matthew 25:37-39

Introduction

1. In this weightiest and most disturbing of all parables, no words are more penetrating, or more arresting, than these of our text. It is something of a shock to many earnest Christians, to learn that when all is said about justification by faith and salvation by believing on Jesus, the final judgment will turn after all upon the *fruits* of saving faith in loving deeds. What you have done, or not done, to the least of these His brethren — that is the decisive question.

2. But our text goes further even than this, and suggests that we are to be finally judged by the things we do, or do not do, *unconsciously*. "Lord, when did we...." It is not just that the speakers have forgotten — few of us forget whatever good we do! We will have time

and date and details ready for the Lord! But here, judgment rests upon what was done or not done without realizing it. Truly, a sobering thought: a man's real influence, real significance to his friends and to society, and his real worth to God, are all unconscious to himself.

3. If Paul was the greatest of all apostles, and his conversion the supreme event of the apostolic age, it is striking to recall that the evangelist concerned, who by his words and life, his courage and death, haunted Saul of Tarsus to the gates of Damascus — the martyr Stephen — died without knowing this victory he had won. If in glory the Lord's "Well done!" recalled the fruit of Stephen's witness, he too could only reply, "Lord, when . . . ?"

I. The unconscious effect of a man's life often strikes deepest.

A. The effect, the influence, we strive after is often spoiled by the striving. So the attempts of parents to influence their children sometimes fail through their very eagerness and concern. So, too, the conversion we pray for and laboriously plan is so often made less likely by our very contriving: we blunder through too great zeal. Yet, other results we scarcely sought fall with delicious surprise into our laps. All unaware, we speak most clearly by our silence, and testify most loudly by being just ourselves.

B. Professor Henry Drummond, Scottish biologist, geologist, and university evangelist, reshaped countless lives by word and pen; yet among the greatest tributes paid at his death was the testimony — said to be echoed by hundreds — that he was the most Christlike man they had known; "to write his biography was like writing the history of a fragrance." That effect on others cannot be organized.

C. Longfellow once held pride of place in American literature; the still more eminent, but aged and now forgetful Emerson stood beside Longfellow's grave to pay tribute, and said: "I forget his name, but the gentleman we are burying today was a sweet and beautiful soul." Such fame cannot be planned for.

D. Of still another, his biographer declared: "He had ever a smile in his eye and laughter in his heart; his coming into any company was like the lifting of blinds and the opening of windows. He lighted fires in all the cold rooms of life." That kind of memory cannot be *managed,* or arranged for.

E. A London laborer said of his fellow laborer, "I never saw him cross the common without feeling better for it." A young man suddenly appeared at a Church in Peckham, attending regularly, seemingly without contact or introduction; in due course the minister asked what brought him there, and was told, "I am working with someone who goes to a Methodist Church, and I thought I would like to know a place which produced people like him."

F. A young missionary recruit fell into despondency and frustration. Homesick, disappointed, feeling inadequate, he returned home. In a few weeks he received a letter from his colleagues: "When you left, it seemed as though the flag was lowered and the music stopped."

G. None of this is the influence that care and forethought can deliberately contrive. Training and careful preparation, eloquence and efficient organization, have little to do with it. It is the unconscious overflow of true souls living in love with Christ. But it strikes deep.

II. The unconscious effect of a man's life often lasts longest.

A. Everyone remembers the story of David Livingstone; returning to the coast of Africa after a long and exhausting inland trek, to find a destroyer awaiting him, at the express instructions of the English Queen, with a royal invitation to travel home in luxury and honor. He weighed the recognition of a Queen against the solemnity of a promise given to his native bearers to see them safely back to their own villages — and turned again into the forest. Not everyone knows the sequel. H. W. Nevinson, a great English journalist, trekking through central Africa years later, wanted to hire a score of native bearers, but lacked money or cloth with which to pay them. He could only promise them wages at the end of the trek — and was astonished to find no shortage of volunteers. "Because," the record says, "he was in Livingstone country": the tradition of honesty, faithfulness, and the white man's promise still lingered. The character of Livingstone remained a moral capital upon which others could draw.

B. A young missionary candidate was asked by the interviewing committee to relate what had quickened her life and led her to offer for service overseas. She had been reared in a good, but only temperately religious family, and a fashionable Church, neither knowing nor feeling much of the depth of spiritual experience. Traveling to town each day by the same train created a friendship with a happy, vivacious, alert and courteous girl from the same district. But each day's journey ended in minutes of silence, as the friend took out her Testament and read her passage for the day. "Soon I wanted," said the candidate, "to be just like her. She invited me sometimes to her Church . . . and the rest has followed." *That* story has not finished yet.

III. The unconscious effect of a man's life stretches immeasurably.

A. A young lad sat in the British House of Commons listening to John Bright's overwhelming eloquence, and went home resolved to become a lawyer. On the day before he was to sign his contract, he met on his home-city streets his old Sunday school teacher — long unnamed and unremembered now. The lad announced excitedly his legal ambitions; he was met with the steadying reply, "That's a great profession; but, Henry, I always hoped you would be a minister of

Christ." He went home silent, and in solitude that night — he has recorded — J. H. Jowett "heard the call of the eternal ringing in the chambers of my soul as clearly as the morning bell in the valleys of Switzerland" — and in Britain and later in New York he exercised a ministry hardly rivaled in this century. But the Sunday school teacher never knew how far his words would echo.

B. One especially dramatic illustration of the far-stretching influence of true testimony is an old Puritan book of 200 years ago, *The Bruised Reed*. Its author is unknown, and he died unaware that his work was noticed. But an Anglican pastor, Richard Baxtor, read it, and was brought to a new experience of Christ. It prompted him to write, and he produced *A Call to the Unconverted* — hardly a title to rock the bookstalls. Yet Philip Doddridge, great leader of the nonconformists in England, read Baxter's book, was deeply moved, and wrote *The Rise and Progress of Religion in the Soul* — one of the world's great religious books. William Wilberforce read this, to his own and the world's great enrichment, and under its inspiration he produced *A Practical View of Christianity*. Thomas Chalmers read this, and went out to set all Scotland ablaze . . . And so it goes on. *And neither writer knew!*

C. Few lives have cast longer shadows, however, than did Lord Shaftesbury's. When his body was carried through London in 1885, tens of thousands stood in pouring rain and thousands wept openly. From the age of 25, though born into wealth and rank, Shaftesbury had fought for children working 12 and 16 hours a day in mines and factories, for the climbing chimney boys, for the Ragged Schools for the poor, for the orphaned and oppressed and underprivileged of every kind, while countless Bible societies, missionary societies, and Christian causes had his active and generous support. None can measure the stretch of such a life. But whence came its spring? Not, we are told, from home and family — immersed in a round of social occasions; but from a humble servant girl in that great household, Maria Millis. She taught the young lord to read his Bible, and how to pray, and "stamped upon his young mind the character of Christ." To the end of his life Lord Shaftesbury carried every day the watch she gave him with her blessing. But she, again, could never know how very far her simple, unconscious influence would spread.

Conclusion

1. It might be said that this recital of instances is neither useful (since unconscious influence is beyond our effort or control), nor entirely encouraging — since it works for evil as for good. The essential truth, however, is that *being* is so much more important than *doing*; and that the unconscious bearing, attitude, mood, and gesture reveal the inner self as few deliberate and guarded actions can. "Lord, when did we

. . .?" might well receive the answer, "You were this, and this, and this, *all the time. . . ."*

2. Hence the supreme importance in Christian living of the cultivation of the soul. Thinking, discussing, planning, organization, effort — all have place; but what you *are* is prior to what you *do;* and so meditation, reading, fellowship, prayer, and worship are prime preoccupations of the disciple who knows that his unconscious self is his real self, all the time. *Be* true, and clean, and gentle and Christlike — and the impact of what you are will be deeper, more lasting, more widely stretched, than anything you can ever contrive to perform.

3. And the Lord will pass by all the deliberate, conscious activities as so much window-dressing and self-promotion, and pinpoint the real fruit of our lives; . . . and we, bewildered, shall ask, "Lord, when . . .?"

34. *The Paradoxical Samaritan*

"A Samaritan . . . came to where he was. . . ." —Luke 10:33

Introduction

1. Every Sunday school boy knows that the Samaritan was "good," and why. The real question, though, is how the priest and Levite (a religious "layman") ever got into the story: their presence is quite unnecessary to Christ's point. And why was the only decent character in the tale a *Samaritan* — on a Jewish road?

2. The strange setting and elaboration of the story are of course quite deliberate. To us "the good Samaritan" has become a symbol of kindly Christian good nature, evoking small acts of good neighborliness. Originally, he was an awkward character in a provocative story invented by Jesus to caricature common attitudes of "good" people. Jesus contrived a politico-religious cartoon, outrageous and explosive to His contemporaries; we make of it a children's address full of sentiment, universalism, and idealism!

3. Hence the need to reread the too-familiar parable, with the actual situation of that time before our minds and the actual needs of our time in our hearts. Then we shall note —

I. How the sentiment dissolves in the ruthlessness of the telling.

A. All the urgent problems of Palestinian Judaism are in this tale. Religious institutionalism grown irrelevant to the real woes of society; an intense piety that was nevertheless no *earthly* good; self-righteousness entirely careless of those who fail to be righteous; racial bitterness erected into religious principle; the wealthy and privileged — despising, yet needing, the outcast and oppressed. It is truly astonishing how up-to-date that list of problems still appears.

B. And where history, tradition, prejudice, religion, and pride, acting and interacting together, had fashioned an "insoluble" problem of human relations — between Jew and Samaritan — the unembittered humanity of the ill-used Samaritan succeeded in bridging it. No form of words or formula of compromise was propounded; no academic questions, as to Samaritan origins, or the right place to worship, or the extent of Samaritan scriptures or the right of the Samaritans to be in Israel, were even discussed! Jesus sharply mocks at all the outstanding issues and the heat they generated, when he drags in the priest, to show him passing by the real problem; and the religious layman, to show him interested, but unmoved, by the real need — holding an inquiry but postponing action! — and focuses on the one simple and realistic re-action — a "pagan's"!

C. No wonder the inquiring lawyer was silenced, and the bystanders astounded, by so obvious and unanswerable a definition of love for one's neighbor! And by such realism. For it is not religious sentiment that will save society or solve its problems, but religious realism; not high-flown talk about first principles, but direct actions expressing common humanity and honest concern.

D. Christian aid and active compassion are the sole practical policy for the racial, historical, political, and religious estrangements that be-devil modern society as they did the Palestine Jesus knew. Theoretic formulae of coexistence have neither meaning nor use except as subsequent records of an active movement of goodwill that created fellowship and ministered to need before the appropriate words were found. How sorely we need that ruthless, impatient realism of Jesus!

Rereading the parable, note too —

II. How the universalism crystallizes into narrowest individualism.

A. On this busy Jericho road, amid uncountable instances of Jewish-Samaritan hatred, one bleeding man lying alone represents the whole problem: and one compassionate heart represents the only solution. Ideologies cure nothing. A Stoic would have pitched this story in grandly universalistic terms, talking of "a common world soul" emerging in this microcosmic situation. A scientific humanist would have moralized on nature's common struggle for existence, on man's common ancestry breeding enthusiasm for (abstract) humanity. Only Jesus makes it one man bending over another man. He always individualizes relentlessly.

B. So a missionary doctor bending over an African leper, a gentle white nurse comforting an Indian mother in labor, *have solved* the racial problem. H. E. Fosdick says somewhere, perceptively, that the problem is not merely evaded but distorted in

> *The little black baby that rolls in the sand*
> *In a country far over the sea,*
> *Is my African brother, and Jesus loves him,*
> *Just as He loves you and me*

because it makes the whole question of inter-racial relationships long-range, global, and impersonal. Jesus *never* lets us generalize. In His way of thinking, world problems, hunger, malnutrition, fear, affliction, homelessness, statelessness are always personalized — one individual lying by the roadside *is* the problem — he does not merely "represent" the problem, as we commonly say. It is permissible to multiply him, till the many individuals in need are realized; but Jesus will not let us theorize him — till the personal pain and peril are forgotten in the "problem."

C. So for the truly Christian "universalist," suffering will always have a personal name, a numbered bed in a particular ward in an identifiable hospital or camp. And the "sufferer" will not care, or even understand, that Christ is the universal Saviour, and Christianity a world religion, if he himself lies neglected, and dies uncomforted. Universal compassion is a sorry sham, an evasive abstraction, until localized, channeled, organized and focused upon living people in Christian action.

Rereading the parable, note finally —

III. How the idealism solidifies into most unromantic concreteness.

A. Not only the *objects* of our compassion and care are deliberately personalized by Jesus; the compassion and care themselves are materialized in the most forthright way. Always Jesus thrusts before us immediate, concrete need — rarely does He talk of love, or kindness, or sympathy: much more often it is of cups of cold water, food for the hungry, clothes for the naked, and the touch of the hand and the physical presence at the bedside of the sick.

B. Here, it is obvious, neither the curiosity of the Levite, nor even the compassion and magnanimity of the Samaritan, heal anything. Oil, wine, robes torn for bandages, conveyance, and two pence do what mere kindly feelings or indignation about the unsafe condition of the roads would never do. At least one apostolic reader understood the parable so: "If any one has the world's goods, and sees his brother in need, yet closes his heart against him, how does God's love abide in him? Little children, let us not love in word or speech but in deed and truth" (I John 3:17, 18).

C. Much hot air circulates in the churches, and spills into the religious weeklies, about "international problems," "Christ the clear solution of world questions," and similar generalized assertions of unassailable orthodoxy and good intention; what the situation actually calls for may be manhandled into a packing-case shipped to a mission field, erected into a hospital or school, enshrined in a medical-missions candidate, an X-ray unit, a brighter ward, a pile of schoolbooks, or just pure water. The Samaritan did not theorize, or emotionalize: he took the patient to an inn. We may need rather to take the inn to the patient. But either way, it is always in the concrete, timely, material *deed* that the non-Christian world glimpses eternal love.

35. *Men of the Word*

"The scribes . . . sit on Moses' seat; so practice and observe whatever they tell you, but not what they do." —Matthew 23:2, 3

Introduction

1. The essence of real tragedy lies not in great disasters, which may be accident, wickedness, or folly; nor in the inevitable nemesis which attends upon deliberate evil; but in the defects of great qualities, which work a man's undoing partly by his very strength; and in the slow decline of high principles into sad failure, because other equally important principles were ignored. Thus the ardent revolutionary, fighting for his people's freedom, becomes a tyrant almost against his will; and the man who has seen one religious truth and follows it wholeheartedly may end in bigotry and fanaticism because of his zeal.
2. Something of this tragic quality marks the career of the Pharisees — originally the Puritans, evangelicals, missionaries of Judaism, but later its most self-righteous and hypocritical representatives — but even more, of the *scribes,* men of a strictly Biblical religion, who ended by opposing, and helping to crucify, the living Word of God.
3. A solemn — and difficult — lesson for all lovers of scripture is enshrined in this story.

I. The strength of Biblical religion

A. In years of Babylonian exile, lacking Temple or king to focus the nation's unity, Jews assembled their sacred literature to help preserve the people's identity and nourish their faith. After the return, when prophecy was rare, or silenced, attention turned to written law for constitution, creed, code of behavior, framework of education. Israel, too, "became a people of a Book, and that Book the Bible."

B. Inevitably, those who understood, copied and interpreted the law became a powerful class, professional men of thorough training and considerable skill; holding seats in the Sanhedrin, receiving honor above that paid to parents. Sitting "in Moses' seat," they advised, taught, sat as arbitrators, served as magistrates and judges; they guided synagogue worship, issued pronouncements as to right or wrong, "bound or loosed" precepts.

C. For the most part, they were devoted men. Theirs was emphatically a religion of the scriptures. Years of patient, exact scholarship stored prodigious learning about what was written; each verse expounded with the wealth of previous opinions, all learned by heart lest another written record should ever rival the sacred page. Phenomenal memories, untiring diligence, meticulous faithfulness, unquestioning obedience were given by the scribes to the written word of God: if sometimes vain of knowledge, they had much to be vain about! Never has scripture received deeper homage.

D. Scribes saw religion supremely in terms of conduct, morals, obedience. Religion was right-doing; not ritual, mystic experiences, right theology, but obedience to the will of God. So concerned that law be faithfully kept, they "hedged" it about with still more rigorous rules ("the tradition of the Elders") lest by negligence or accident any should disobey unaware. This emphasis upon right conduct is one of the finest elements in the scribal type of piety; it helped to make Jewish morality the envy of the pagan world. *Revelation* and *rectitude* are still foundations of a Bible-loving faith.

II. The dangers of legalistic devotion to the Book

A. It was therefore the greater tragedy that these devotees of Book-religion and moral law should have led in crucifying Jesus.

B. But Jesus sharply criticized this scriptural legalism. It made religion burdensome, narrow, miserable, restrictive; its watchword was, "You must not"; its creed, "God will judge"; its sorest lack, any comfort for the stricken or hope for the sinner. It forgot, too, that there is more to right action than outward deed: the spirit in which a thing is done, the motive, the intention behind the act, help to determine its moral quality. A man is good or bad *at heart,* as well as before the law.

C. That failure to see beneath external appearance led to hypocrisy. If a thing was not actually forbidden by the letter of the law, then too often it was held "permissible," though it broke the *intention* of a dozen other laws. Widows might be robbed of homes, parents deprived of support by sons, *within the forms of law,* by appealing to some disconnected precept, and a final "It is written. . . ."

D. And scribal piety got things sadly out of proportion; it "strained out gnats" of conscientious scruples; "swallowed whole camels" of injustice, sharp practice, common human unkindness. All book-religion tends to zeal about details — buying stamps on Sunday, right views about Advent program, meaning of the High Priest's vestments, interpretation of the Tabernacle — and yet manages sometimes to be spiteful, slanderous, underhanded, plain dishonest, without noticing!

E. It was part of the tragedy of Calvary that men so earnest, so devoted to the Word of God and to the law of right, should help to crush the Christ of God. His disregard for pious regulations, His free friendship for outcast and lawless, His claim to speak with God's authority a new and living word, angered them deeply. As traditionalists, conservatives, men of *written* word alone, all revelation seemed to them to lie within a safe, and distant, past. Their God was the God of the past; their obedience a devotion to authority in the past. Jesus (and before Him, John the Baptist), came with a *novel* inspiration, a new, life-giving message, speaking not by accumulated authority of innumerable gathered opinions, but by the Spirit of timeless truth: and the men of the word cried, "Blasphemy!"

F. A religion only of the past, without God of the present age; a devotion to written truth, deaf to the living voice of God today; a religion of right conduct, without knowledge of the human heart or hope of forgiveness for the penitent; a religion of rules that knows no freedom, of regulations that leave no room for inspiration — such always opposes the free, glad, onward-moving Spirit of Jesus, blowing where it listeth.

And as the scribes themselves would say, "Whatsoever things were written aforetime were written for our learning. . . ."

36. *How Prayer Is Answered* 3/98

"Have no anxiety about anything, but in everything by prayer and supplication with thanksgiving, let your requests be made known to God. . . . My God will supply every need of yours according to his riches in glory in Christ Jesus." —Philippians 4:6, 19

Introduction

1. There are no better arguments for prayer than the answers received, and these Jesus plainly promises. "Your Father, who hears in secret, will reward you. . . . Everyone that asketh . . . seeketh . . . knocketh . . . receiveth, findeth, it is opened." Sometimes, however, as much spiritual discernment is required to appreciate the answer as to offer the prayer. God so often does not only more than we ask but *differently.*

2. A shipwrecked sailor prayed fervently and believingly, night after night, for help, protection, courage, deliverance; he returned to camp one evening to find his only shelter ablaze, all his equipment destroyed. Thrown into passionate grief and despair, unable to pray again, he sobbed himself asleep — to be awakened by a rescue party from a distant ship attracted by the fire! An ancient Hebrew tale makes the same point. A rabbi traveling in dangerous countryside with a donkey, a lamp, and a hen to provide eggs, uncomplainingly bowed to God's will when the donkey bolted, the lamp blew out, and the hen died. In the morning he discovered that marauding soldiers had passed within yards; who would certainly have killed him if the donkey had brayed, the light betrayed his presence, or the hen clucked! Even when God grants what we ask, there is no reason why He must grant it in our way.

3. But the full truth is that, given any earnest, thoughtful, and unselfish prayer, one of at least three things may happen:

I. **God may change the situation about which we pray.**

A. In Acts 12:5-17 Peter is in prison, and every circumstance locks him in — he is in the inner ward, bound, lying between two soldiers, with others on guard, beyond an iron gate, and he himself is asleep! Yet God got him out. The early Christians found it as hard to believe that direct divine intervention as we do (see verses 15, 16); yet they had been praying!

B. In Acts 4:23-29 the Church in great distress prays concerning the pressure of persecution; they ask for courage, boldness, vindication. God in answer converts the persecutor — and again the Church is dumbfounded (Acts 9:26).

C. In Acts 16:19f. Paul and Silas in prison in Philippi pray and sing, "shaking heaven by the hems," as Francis Thompson would say. The outcome is an earthquake that shakes jail and jailor, magistrates and city out of their wits!

D. Yet these are only dramatic examples of an experience every Christian knows — right decisions are reached; money is provided; solutions "present themselves"; obstacles are overcome, or melt away, or present themselves as unexpected opportunities; the attitudes of others suddenly change. Surprising, inexplicable, humbling things happen, to rebuke our want of faith. Over and over again, the prayerful prove that "if a thing is right it should be done, and if it should it can."

E. For prayer is the request of instructed and disciplined hearts to a Father in whose hands are all the corners of the earth and all the powers and resources within it. God the Maker and Ruler of the earth, who intervened in history in Christ, remains mighty and free within His world: life and its situations, things and their laws, persons and their decisions, remain subject to God the all-disposing. Therefore

104

prayer offered to Him as He bids may well change our situation, to our perpetual surprise.

II. Or God may show us how to change the situation while we pray.

A. We cry, "Lord, do this or that!" and sometimes the answer comes, "Do it yourself!" Often we pray that God will do what He has commanded us to do: evangelize the world, feed the hungry, unite His people, bend our stubborn wills. Often too we ask for things — blessing, power, joy, success in some Christian enterprise, forgiveness — to be given us as *gifts*, when His word has made plain that these can be ours only upon clear conditions. The right answer to our prayer is often a command.

B. Joshua prayed earnestly, heart-brokenly, at Ai concerning Israel's defeat before the Canaanites (Joshua 7:6-12). He received the pre-emptory reply, "Arise, why have you thus fallen on your face? Israel has sinned . . ." and instructions for investigation and judgement.

C. Moses pleads with God at the impasse of the Red Sea, with the waves before, the desert on either side, the Egyptian pursuit behind; again the divine answer is stern — "Why do you cry to me? Tell the people of Israel to go forward" (Exodus 14:15).

D. Paul, on his second missionary journey, met closed doors, ill health, and forbidding motions of the Spirit that evidently perplexed his mind and clouded his prayers — until the vision at Troas of the man of Macedonia transformed frustration into opportunity by *commanding Paul to act* (Acts 16:6-10). His situation is not changed for him: he is shown how to transform it.

D. It is possible that when Peter inquired about the needed tax payment (Matthew 18:24-27) the reply of Jesus about finding a coin in the fish's mouth really meant "Go and earn the thing you ask for!" At any rate, Jesus *would* sometimes say that. Prayer is never a substitute for obedience, or effort, or thinking. It is of no use at all to pray in order to evade plain duty. Yet, "Why have you fallen on your face . . . ? Tell the people to go forward . . . . Come over and help us . . ." *are* answers to prayer. Whenever the condition of blessing is made clear through prayer, whenever the right action is made compulsive in our hearts, that new insight and impulse, and the blessing that results, are still gracious gifts of the God who answers prayer.

III. Or God may leave the situation as it is and change the one who prays.

A. This may be the hardest answer to prayer for us to recognize, or to accept. Lying in prison, Paul the tireless apostle and evangelist was frustrated, fettered, apparently useless. He himself, and the whole Philippian Church, prayed earnestly against this waste of talent and of burning faith. But Paul transforms the whole position by seizing the opportunity to witness to Christ among the soldiery, in the court, to his wardens and fellow prisoners. So he can write (Philippians 1:12-26) that the whole situation has turned out for the furtherance of the gospel — but the key to that result lay in his own attitude and response, the fruit of prayer.

B. The same is true of his protracted and frustrating illness, the stake or thorn in the flesh against which he thrice prayed "unsuccessfully." The outcome, in understanding and "grace sufficient," in resignation and consequent increase of spiritual power, are all changes within the heart and attitude of Paul. The outward circumstances remain apparently unaltered; but the reaction bred of prayer transforms their whole effect, and brings the longed-for good out of the resented evil.

C. It happens that three prisoners of more modern times teach us the same lesson. Bunyan made the enforced silence and inactivity of Bedford jail yield for him and for God not a bitter complaint and a sulky fatalism, but a masterpiece of evangelical teaching and appeal in *Pilgrim's Progress*. Samuel Rutherford, exiled and restrained (though not literally imprisoned) in Aberdeen, instead of railing against his enforced inactivity and silence wrote some of the loveliest meditations and letters in Christian history. And Dietrich Bonhoeffer, rejecting bitterness and despair, penned for our time a correspondence full of hope and searching challenge, much of whose value is still to be discovered. The man who prays adjusts to circumstances and sufferings, finding them no longer a problem or a barrier: tensions are resolved, antagonisms die, resentments and bitterness are healed. The thing prayed about may remain unchanged: the praying makes the prayer different — and the outcome good.

Conclusion

It is a brave, perceptive, far-seeing faith that sings:

> *Hast thou not seen*
> *How thine entreaties have been*
> *Granted in what He ordaineth?*

But surely it does not matter *how* God answers prayer: we know He does, and that's enough.

37. *It's God's World*

A Harvest Sermon

"The earth is the Lord's and the fullness thereof, the world and those who dwell therein. . . ." —Psalm 24:1

Introduction

1. Few occasions of worship are as old, or as widespread, as "Harvest Festival," by whatever name described. The Bible places the idea very early, in its fourth chapter; underlines its obligation in tithes and other offerings; prescribes its enduring meaning in the festival of the first-fruits; and repeatedly recalls men to the truths it enshrines. And in pagan religions likewise, the natural man is everywhere conscious of the relation of worship to the crowning season of the year.

2. The note of the festival is, traditionally, thanksgiving; and gratitude is a valid obligation. But more than the recognition of divine goodness is involved. We assert here the *unity of things*: we declare that worship and work, God and nature, heaven and the soil, belong together; that streets, fields, markets, schools, senates, workshops, sea, and distant stars are all God's, made, upheld, controlled by the God and Father of our Lord Jesus Christ. We are saying more than "Thank you, God, for everything"; we assert that "The earth is the Lord's . . ." in every sense.

I. The earth is the Lord's.

A. We assert this *against the arrogant, defiant heresy* that the earth is man's — to rule, remake, share out, defile; that man is lord of all he surveys, with unlimited power at his disposal and only his own unbridled ambition to serve — his urge to dominate, defy, and destroy. Moderns forget that man is a creature of six dozen years, puny, frail, mortal — a mere sheep under God's hand. This human pride is fundamental to most modern problems —

If the earth is man's, all hope of security lies in achieving a precarious balance of human interests; that is, in the interest of the strongest. Then might is right.

If the earth is the Lord's, all hope lies in doing what God counts right; in the long run, right is might.

The festival of each year's Fall reasserts man's *tenancy* and *dependence* in a world that is always *God's*.

107

B. We assert this *against the faithless, despairing heresy* that the earth is the devil's and so nothing can save it or improve it. The man of God may wash his hands of it, for it is doomed. There is some truth in this somewhere; but as an excuse for inaction it is a betrayal of God's kingdom. The earth is God's, where His reign must be acknowledged, His will done as in heaven. God loved it, and gave His Son to be its Saviour. At Harvest, we refuse to join the rebellious conspiracy; we *reclaim* the earth for God, as His by right of creation and of redemption.

C. We assert this *against the compromising, divisive heresy* that shares earth between God and the devil, the hoary half-truth that *parts* of the earth are the Lord's — sacred groves, altars, smoking mountains, hilltops, springs, shrines, temples, bits of "consecrated ground" — on Israel's land but not her neighbors'. There is a place for reverence towards a site or building reserved for worship, or associated with some sacred event; but not for that exclusive consecration which *confines* God to such places and leaves all others "secular" — and unhallowed, unsurrendered. To the truly consecrated man, all earth is consecrated ground.

Our Harvest worship asserts this down-to-earth faith: the world is God's, alive with God, linked to God, dependent upon God, and answerable to God.

II. The fullness of the earth is the Lord's.

A. The general truth, that the earth is the Lord's, takes on at Harvesttime this special and particular emphasis, that the fruits, the produce, the wealth of the world, is also the Lord's. With all man's cleverness, he cannot make grass, soil, sunshine or seed, nor create livestock, raw materials, or the basic elements of matter. All wealth and welfare, all civilization, knowledge, and life rest ultimately on gifts of God, the Giver of all good.

B. With exquisite appropriateness, this Psalm was appointed to be sung in the Jewish Temple on the first day of each working week, as the Jew returned from his Sabbath rest to the daily tasks of preparing, increasing, distributing, and using the gifts of God. He was thus reminded, forcibly, that only they can worship acceptably, can ascend the hill of the Lord and stand in His holy place, who return from the market, the workshop, and the fields, with *clean hands,* unsoiled by any sordid dishonest deal; with *pure hearts,* uncorrupted by any deceitful love of gain that has over-reached their neighbors; who *have not lifted up their souls* in worship of vain idols of riches or ambition; who *have not used the divine name to swear falsely* about their bargains, contracts, and engagements. So the Hebrew poet had forthrightly interpreted the kind of daily reverence due from godly hearts toward the "raw materials of commerce," as gifts of the good God. The Royal Exchange at Cornhill, London, for many years the center of London's grain trade, bears on its present building the same declaration — "The earth is the Lord's" — with the same intention: that men trading in God's gifts might remember that honesty, truth and fair dealing, and unselfish sharing of good things, is more than business ethics — it is simple religion.

C. So again, Harvest worship unifies worship and work; it relates thanksgiving for gifts received with responsibility before God for use made of them. The down-to-earth faith implies a concrete code of everyday behavior, that lifts business relationships into the field of highest piety.

III. The throne of the earth is the Lord's also.

A. At first sight verses 7-10 seem to have little to do with the theme of the Psalm, and it is sometimes conjectured that a fragment from some other poem has been inserted here. Guesses about the special occasion presupposed vary, from the time when David restored the Ark of God (regarded as the Lord's throne) within the new shrine at Jerusalem, to some splendid royal occasion — probably a coronation — or to the annual Feast of Tabernacles, when (it is said) God's chariot was drawn again into the Temple in solemn procession. All this is conjecture; but that *some* such occasion was in mind is fairly certain, and that the final verses were sung alternately by those outside the Temple gates seeking admission, and those inside, ceremonially challenging the right of entry. And the main point is beyond doubt: entry is demanded in the name of the Lord, the "Glorious King" of all. Whether at the first consecration of the Temple, at repeated coronations, or at annual feasts, the nation is clearly reminded of the divine sovereignty. Because the earth is the Lord's, because its fullness belongs to Him alone, He alone is King.

B. This again we declare at Harvest. Written deep into conscience, history, experience, and scripture are principles that guarantee this is *not* a crazy world, governed by chance or accident. There is a moral order, in which man ultimately reaps exactly what he sows. God remains King: His laws may be broken, but they cannot be evaded; His penalties fall slowly, but they are sure; His will may be opposed, but it cannot be defeated. Man struts, and boasts, and defies Him, but God will not yield His realm to violent, ambitious, unscrupulous men. He is the King of Glory.

Such is the message of each Fall festival: the world is God's — its every part, its contents, its future, its people, and you and I. We worship our Maker, Provider, and King; and we promise to make our daily work consistent with our worship.

38. *"I am the Way"*

"I am the way, and the truth, and the life; no one comes to the Father, but by me." —John 14:6

Introduction

Out of a conversation conducted, it seems, at cross-purposes, emerges one of the greatest conceivable claims to fall from any lips. Jesus has spoken in terms of an imminent separation, and Peter asks, "Lord, where are you going?" Jesus breaks the truth to them gently, in stages: "Where you cannot follow yet . . . to the Father's house . . . to where I shall presently bring you." Thomas would appear not to have been listening: he asks, "We know not where . . . how can we know the way?" And Jesus answers with the stupendous words: "I am the way."

I. The threefold meaning of the claim

A. *He is the way to the knowledge of the Father.*

1. Philip's plea seems to mean, "The Father — Lord, who is He? Show us the Father." This is the cry of the religious heart in every generation. Every faith, philosophy, mysticism, "mystery-religion," and theosophy professes to conduct men into "Reality," to unveil the inner secrets of things. Their persistence and popularity express man's thirst for such understanding, man's need for revelation. This Jesus too describes: "No man hath seen God. . . . No man knows the Father save the Son . . . and he to whom the Son shall reveal Him."

2. Set thus against the universal ignorance, longing, and rival claims, the declaration "He that hath seen me hath seen the Father" is truly breath-taking. Without Christ, there is no full and final knowledge of God. With Him, there is no room or need for agnosticism.

Christ is *the way for the mind:* He *enlightens* us about God.

B. *He is the way to the presence of the Father.*

1. For Jesus speaks at once of our "coming" to the Father. The immediate background, for Jewish readers, would be the strict prohibitions within the Temple against intrusion beyond prescribed limits — set differently for Gentiles and women, for laymen and for priests. The veil of the Temple hung before the sacred place, and beyond the ordinary worshiper was admitted only *representatively,* in the High Priest. From Sinai onwards, the Jewish worshiper was required to "keep his distance." John's pagan readers would have in mind the no less for-

110

bidding ideas of the Greek "Mysteries," the almost inaccessible deities and secret rites of the pagan temples, and the occult initiation ceremonies, or Gnostic secrets, by which experience of the divine was offered to those willing to undergo the prescribed disciplines.

2. Against all such ideas, the gospel invites men to come to God, freely, directly, immediately, through a new and living way opened up for us by Christ.

> We have obtained access to this grace wherein we stand (Romans 5:2). Through Him we both have access by one Spirit unto the Father, We have . . . confidence of access, through our faith (Ephesians 2:18; 3:12).

Christ is our High Priest, our Advocate, and our Mediator — the religious, legal, and political metaphors all mean the same: in Him and through Him we have *access to God,* entrance, invitation, and welcome. In Him we draw near; in Him we pray.

Christ is *the way for the heart:* He *conducts* us to God.

C. *He is the way to the Father's House.*

1. This is Christ's immediate meaning: He is returning to the Father, to "Him that sent me." He pioneers the way through death, promising to return, to receive them, to re-gather them "where I am." "If it were not so, I would have told you."

2. This too is to be read against the background of Jewish uncertainties about the afterlife — Sadducean doubts, the Old Testament's ambiguities; and against the background (for John's other readers) of pagan ignorance and superstition, the "mysteries" and charms and incantations affirmed to give guidance in the next life. Compare, for example, the Egyptian "Book of the Dead," with its instructions and directions for the soul's way into the underworld: Jesus gives, instead, leadership and companionship.

Christ is *the way for the spirit:* He *brings us home* to God.

No claim could be more audacious, or exciting. It plainly implies a more-than-human status, authority, and nature. Only He whose rightful place is in the bosom of the Father *could* so "declare Him."

II. The threefold measure of the claim

A. *The Truth.*

1. The great claim is still more greatly emphasized as Jesus offers Himself as *the* Truth — a meaning which is implied even if the right translation is "true and living way." Only right thinking about God can generate a true experience of Him, for we can never experience what we do not know. The darkness of pagan ignorance and error was thus a fatal stumblingblock to a right relationship with God; and even in Judaism, the narrow legalist and nationalist conception of God current in some circles set severe limits upon what men could experience of His boundless grace. So the light of Christ's revelation of the

Father was, and is, a necessary prerequisite to the Christian experience of salvation.

2. This emphasis upon true knowledge of God is characteristic of John's gospel. "If thou knewest . . . thou wouldest have asked . . . and he would have given. . . ." (4:10); "this is eternal life, that they might know Thee. . . ." (17:3); "ye shall know the truth, and the truth shall set you free" (8:32): such verses show that *prayer, life*, and *freedom* are conditioned by right understanding, such as Christ has come to give (I John 5:20).

3. As the true "image" of God, the "Son" who alone knows the Father, and the Word which was from the beginning with God, *Jesus* can reveal that understanding, because He is Himself the Truth. This is the first step of the "Way" — belief of the truth Christ brings: we leave all false, misleading ways and step out upon the way of true understanding, when we *believe* in Christ.

> *Thou art my way: I wander if Thou fly . . .*
> *My path is lost; my wandering steps do stray;*
> *I cannot safely go, nor safely stay;*
> *Whom should I seek but Thee, my Path, my Way?*

B. *The Life.*

1. Yet Christ's way is emphatically a way of living, not merely of thinking. The Old Testament frequently offers two ways — of wisdom or folly, of righteousness or sin, of God or evil, and demands that we choose the right way. Jesus too spoke of the broad and narrow ways, that lead to life or death. The earliest epithet for the gospel prescription for living is "the Way" — five times in Acts that is a sufficient description of Christianity. Lao Tse in China was hailed as "Lord of the Way"; Buddha in India pointed men to his "Eightfold Path." Throughout these expressions the same conception recurs: men need a path, an unerring map of life, a route-finder and a guide, to direct safely and without waste of years or strength the daily conduct and work that make up our *life*. Christ claims *in that sense* to be our *Life* — Example, Pattern, Master, and Guide, leading forth His sheep into safety and green pasture, calling us to follow Him along the path of life.

2. Christ is, however, not only the pattern of our life, but also its power. It is the glory of the gospel to be able to offer, not only the map and the route and the guide to right conduct, but the spiritual resources, the inspiration, faith, and hope, the moral courage and spiritual strength, and the new birth of human nature itself by repentance and the Spirit (John 3), which make the ideal pattern *possible*. "Christ . . . is our life" (Colossians 3:4) — Christ in us the hope of glory. God has given to us eternal life, and this life is in His Son (I John 5:11). He not only shows us the way, but walks it with us: "Christ liveth in me . . . the life that I live I live by faith of the Son of God . . ." (Galatians 2:20).

3. Nothing less than this can adequately express Christ's meaning in this claim, or His meaning in our lives. He is our "life" — the life we are called to live, and the life by which we live: the *true way* of *life*.

C. *The Way.*

1. Even yet we have not taken full measure of Christ's claim, for He immediately adds, "No man cometh unto the Father but by me." This can only mean that He is more than a way of living: He is the way to the Father, and the *only* way — no man comes any other.

2. This is the enduring "scandal" of the gospel: the offensive exclusiveness of Christianity. But it is unavoidable. If the gospel be true at all, rival ideas that contradict it *must* be untrue. If Christ be the Truth . . . all contrary ideas must be false; if He be the Life, to be without Him, or against Him, must be death; if He be the Way, to wander elsewhere is to be lost. That there is some truth — not contrary to Christ's — gleaming here and there in the pagan conscience, in the godly half-believing Roman centurion, in the surrounding darkness of the world, Paul (in Romans 1 and 2), Luke (in Acts 10), and John (in John 1) would agree. But He, alone, is the true and living way by which men find the God they seek. "There is none other name, given under heaven among men, whereby we must be saved."

3. In fact, of course, history offers no real rival. Christ is unique; as revelation, as example, as atonement, as resurrection from the dead — however we assess His work, it is unparalleled. For mind, for morality, for experience of acceptance with God, He remains the only true and living Way to the Father.

> *None other Lamb, none other Name,*
> *None other hope in heaven or earth or sea,*
> *None other hiding-place from guilt and shame,*
> *None beside Thee!*

Conclusion

Christ is the Way, to wisdom, goodness, and God. The Way through life, through the world, through our problems; the way out, the way forward, the way home. In every context of need, He is the true and living way, the answer to the cry of a world long *lost*.

Are we on that way, permanently?

Are we treading it, progressively?

39. "I am the Bread of Life"

"I am the bread of life; he who comes to me shall not hunger, and he who believes in me shall never thirst." —John 6:35

Introduction

1. "Man shall not live by bread alone, but by every word that proceeds from the mouth of God," the Jewish Law declared, and Jesus lent to the affirmation His additional authority by quoting it. "So shall my word be," promised a prophet, ". . . seed to the sower and *bread to the eater*."

> *The hunger in man's heart is infinite*
> *And craves infinity for food:*
> *I dare not give man bread unless I give him more —*
> *He must have God.*

is the diagnosis of Studdert Kennedy. And all who understand the human heart concur.

2. Man's spiritual hunger is various, but not vague. Says one observer, "Man hungers to be good, in spite of evil propensities; he hungers to understand the meaning of things; to be comforted in adversity; he longs for peace, righteousness, inspiration, truth, and hope." Despite his occasional denials, man hungers too for the divine; he thirsts, sometimes without knowing it, for God. It is partly by the nature and range of his appetites that man is distinguished from the brutes. The human soul is no more self-sustaining than is the human body: and the starved soul is no less in peril than the starved physical frame.

3. To this varied, universal hunger, native to man's constitution, Christ's claim here is addressed: "I am the bread of life." Its occasion and its form clearly illustrate its relevance and its grace.

I. An instructive comparison

A. The occasion of this great claim was a community meal on seaside slopes above Galilee, after a long day's teaching and questioning. Christ's simple compassion for the crowd's natural hunger, and perhaps a wish to illustrate divine providence in vivid and personal terms, prompted the miracle of the feeding of the thousands. It was a fitting, and grateful, close to a memorable day.

B. But it was more. John (in verse 4), the crowd (verse 31), and Jesus Himself (verse 32) all set this communal meal into the context of the Exodus story of the manna from heaven and water from the rock (John 6:35 adds "he shall never *thirst*"). The season was Passover, and the provision miraculous — that was sufficient to prompt the comparison with ancient story. Moreover, some expected that Messiah when He came, would repeat the manna miracle: there may well be a reference to this in the story of Jesus' temptation (Matthew 4:3); and some expected too that He would reveal where the pot of manna, once preserved within the sacred Ark, had been concealed (see Revelation 2:17). No wonder the people began to make comparisons! Jesus was greater than Moses, "indeed the prophet who is to come" (verse 14). The Messianic prosperity for all was already at hand: they would gladly force Him to become their King (verse 15).

C. Yet this only revealed the shallowness of their hope and understanding. God does indeed supply the need and satisfy the hunger of His pilgrim people; but there is the deeper hunger, and a Bread imperishable (verse 27); there is a Messianic prosperity not of loaves and luxury but of truth and righteousness. There is a spiritual manna, from a spiritual Messiah, nourishing spiritual life. Moses met only the immediate physical need (verse 49); Jesus offers Bread for the life of the soul. Of this nourishment for the eternal craving in the nature of man, the feeding of the five thousand was but an eloquent "sign." Christ is Himself the spiritual banquet that Moses could not offer. Man, however, still prefers to labor hardest for the bread that perishes.

II. A startling contrast

A. Natural though the comparison with Moses was in all the attendant circumstances, it breaks down into sharp contrast once details are attended to. It is not enough to say that Moses could give only physical food, where Jesus offered spiritual (verses 49, 58); or that Moses could only give what God provided, whereas Jesus is Himself Bread for the soul (32). This reveals Christ's immeasurably superior authority — but there is more.

B. The life that Jesus gives, and then sustains, is life *eternal* (verses 27, 50, 58). Four times Jesus reiterates that He will raise at the last day those whom He has nourished:

> This is the will of him that sent me, that I should lose nothing of all that he has given me, but raise it up at the last day (39);

> This is the will of my Father, that every one who sees the Son and believes in him should have eternal life; and I will raise him up at the last day (40);

> No one can come to me unless the Father who has sent me draws him; and I will raise him up at the last day (44);

He who eats my flesh and drinks my blood has eternal life; and I
will raise him up at the last day (54).

The New Testament scarcely contains a finer cluster of promises concerning immortality! The faithfulness of Christ in keeping His own
(39), the sovereign will of the Father who appoints the destiny of
believers (40), the unchallengeable authority of the Father behind
every man's spiritual experience, which death shall not defy (44), and
the inmost, undefinable nourishment of the believer upon the living
Christ (54) are all here urged *by the Master Himself* as guarantees that
we shall live again. Plainly the simple parable, read into and out of
the compassionate miracle, has led on to a startling promise: the life
that feeds upon this living Bread will live for ever.

C. The sharp contrast between Moses' gift and that of Christ as to
its content is matched, inevitably, by equal contrast in *its manner*.
Moses' part was merely to promise, to instruct, to point to the gift of
God and organize its collection. Christ's part is infinitely greater. He
is Himself the living Bread, imparting Himself through faith to every
believer. For this, He, like bread, must be "broken": "the bread which
I shall give for the life of the world is my flesh" (51); "My flesh is
food indeed, and my blood is drink indeed" (55). It is impossible
for us to read these words, as it was impossible for John's original readers, without thinking of the Memorial Supper, with its deep memories
of the breaking of His precious body and the shedding of His precious
blood, that His life yielded in death might bring us life. "Take, eat,
this is my body broken for you . . . this my blood . . ." lends dramatic
commentary to this teaching upon Christ the living sustenance of the
soul. Yet John insists that the "eating" and "drinking" must not be
less than a full

believing in Christ (verse 29, and 35, 36, 40, 47)
seeing Christ — with understanding (36, 40)
coming to Christ (35, 37, 44, 45)
abiding in Christ (56).

Always the Bread is Jesus Himself — not something we can take and
lay upon a table, but the living Lord — given (32), incarnate (33),
broken (51), and assimilated (56). We feed upon Him by faith: only
as our partaking of the Supper expresses and reaffirms this personal
coming in faith to Christ does He then and there nourish the believing
soul with life eternal. "It is the spirit that gives life, the flesh is of
no avail; the words that I have spoken to you are spirit and life" (63).

D. It is little wonder that the Jews listening at Capernaum felt themselves out of their depth: "This is a hard saying; who can listen to it?"
(60). Compassion and providence they could understand; and the
exciting comparisons with Israel's experience in the Exodus wandering
were fruitful cause of whispered conversations and speculation. But
to give and sustain a life eternal, and to do so by the giving and com-
municating of *Himself* — these ideas reached far beyond their com-

prehension. Looking back long afterwards from the height of Christian experience and from the far side of Calvary, John read Christ's meaning, and knew that Peter had spoken truly: "Lord . . . you have the words of eternal life; and we have believed, and have come to know, that you are the Holy One of God" (68, 69).

Conclusion

1. The depth of theological and evangelical meaning in this great chapter, and this great claim, must not hide from us its strong practical importance — both on a social and an individual scale. On a social scale, for example, much depends upon what "feeds the minds" of the rising generation. J. B. Middlebrook, a British missionary leader of exceptionally deep and wide experience, after surveying the emergent situation in India and Pakistan, the rising religious nationalism, the extending democracy and the intense ferment of new ideas that are changing the face of Asia, posed as the crucial question for this decade, "What shall feed the soul of the new East?" It is a momentous query: on what will the ideals, the beliefs and assumptions that shape society, be fed? What shall promote and sustain the social hopes, the professional standards, the vision of writers, poets, and artists, the motives of public service, the national discipline of new states? On what shall the new Asia be nourished? And we may well add, on what is the soul of the West to be nourished? — on denials? on cynicism? on a superficial, "contented-not-to-know" agnosticism? Unless Jesus is the Bread of life to us, our society will perish with spiritual hunger.

2. And so will our souls. In the constant drain of strength and faith and hopefulness which the ceaseless demands and conflicts of modern life impose, some continual refreshment and nourishment are imperative. We need ever and again to prove how He satisfies the longing soul, and fills the hungry with good things.

> 'Twas August, and the fierce sun overhead
> Smote on the squalid streets of Bethnal Green;
> And the pale weaver, through his windows seen
> In Spitalfields, looked thrice dispirited.
>
> I met a preacher there I knew, and said:
> "Ill and o'erworked, how fare you in this scene?"
> "Bravely" said he, "for I of late have been
> Much cheered with thoughts of Christ, the living Bread."
>
> O human soul! as long as thou canst so
> Set up a mark of everlasting light
> Above the howling senses' ebb and flow,
> To cheer thee, and to right thee if thou roam —
> Not with lost toil thou labourest through the night:
> Thou makest the heaven thou hop'st indeed thy home!
>
> (Matthew Arnold)

117

40. "I am the Good Shepherd"

"The good shepherd lays down his life for the sheep." —John 10:11

Introduction

The Rabbis said that "To be a shepherd is next door to being a heathen." They were rough, rugged, ordinary men of the laboring class, with little time for ritual, learning, ceremonial cleansing, so highly valued in Judaism; they were too often away from home to be regular at Temple or synagogue worship, and hence were classed with publicans, sinners, the "people of the land." Sometimes, too, they were mere hirelings — dishonest, cowardly, and faithless. Only the Christmas stories, the Christian haloes, the starlight, and the pathos of lambing-time amid northern snows have sentimentalized this hard-headed occupation, and made romantic men who on occasion were so little trusted as to be held liable in law for the value of any sheep reported "lost." On the other hand, a tried and responsible shepherd might be entrusted with large and very valuable flocks. It is necessary thus to deglamorize "shepherding," to reveal the deep seriousness and the immensity of Christ's claim here — "I am the Good Shepherd."

I. The immense claim to authority

A. John 10 is the direct sequel to John 9, from which no chapter division should have separated it. In 9:34, 35 the Pharisees "excommunicate" (as we would say) the man born blind whom Christ has healed, because of his stubborn defence of Jesus. This official ban was much dreaded: it was held to shut the victim out of Israel, out of the covenant, out of worship, and out of hope. It carried inevitably the stigma of a social outcast, and a divine curse. This is why Jesus diligently seeks him out, to reassure and comfort him: and especially to claim supreme authority over God's fold, as the divinely appointed Shepherd and the Door for the sheep (10:3-5, 7, 16). Those whom Christ admits — like this blind man who believes in Him — none may dare banish: none can pluck them out of the Good Shepherd's hand (28, 29). Admission and banishment are Christ's prerogative alone. Such is His authority.

B. The implied contrast, of course, is with other, self-appointed authorities — false shepherds, hirelings, who have not the welfare of the flock at heart, but only their own interest. Such "cares nothing for the sheep," because they are not his own, but at the moment of danger flees and leaves the sheep to their fate (12, 13). The "good" shepherd, the "true" shepherd, who is a shepherd first and foremost, cares for them to the point of sacrificing his own safety for their protection. It is this *care* and devotion that are at once the basis and the proof of the divine authority of Jesus. The true Shepherd shows the same care as God, the Owner of the flock.

C. In Jewish ears, this charge of falseness and self-seeking against the official shepherds of Israel would echo the grave condemnation voiced by Ezekiel (34:1-10) against national and religious leaders of his day who misused authority and neglected their charge. Ezekiel details a very sharp indictment against the folly, the faithlessness, and the failure of the shepherds whose betrayal of trust had made the Babylonian Exile inevitable. And he prophesies that they shall be replaced, and shamed, as God Himself shall undertake the shepherding of Israel, reclaiming the lost, binding up their wounds, and sheltering the flock within the fold. Moreover, God will raise up "my servant David" — the shepherd-king — to be their shepherd: in him faithful shepherding and wise rule coincide. He is another "good," true, shepherd, and the sign is the faithful exercise of authority. A similar linking of ideas occurs in the Greek version of Isaiah 63:11 (and in certain rabbinic writings) where Moses is called "Shepherd of God's sheep" — with reference to his status as leader of the people.

D. All this lies behind the familiar, gracious word of Jesus to the blind man, and to the crowd, as John reflects upon it afterwards. The Good Shepherd sets the earthly, faithless shepherds aside. He alone has divine authority to admit to God's fold, or to excommunicate. He is the "Chief Shepherd" (I Peter 5:4), whose responsibilities are exercised only for the good of the flock. He is the "Great Shepherd of the sheep" (Hebrews 13:20) who shall lead the flock even from the dead and make them perfect to do God's will. Soberly considered, the claim is immeasurable. It assumes Christ's right to exclusive arbitration of individual destiny. As in the parable of the sheep and goats, the Shepherd sits in judgment — admitting, excluding, by His own authority because He cares enough to die for the sheep.

II. The implicit claim to divinity

A. It cannot be evaded, however, that "Shepherd" is in the last analysis a *divine* title. The whole background of Biblical usage points to this ultimate implication behind Christ's words. The Shepherd of Israel (Psalm 80:1) is the Lord Jehovah. The Shepherd of Psalm 23 is no less certainly the living God. And the Shepherd of Isaiah 40 — who will feed His flock . . . gather the lambs with His arm . . . carry them in His bosom and gently lead those that are with young — is the Lord God omnipotent. In Ezekiel also (chapter 34) the flock is God's, and the ultimate care of it is His delight. The claim of Jesus has this fully in mind, as the references to the Father's hand and to the gift of *eternal* life plainly show. It is no mere metaphor for earthly leadership. So, too, in Revelation 7:15-17 Christ's shepherding is carried into eternal realms, as He shepherds the triumphant dead and leads them to living fountains of waters. There is nothing less implied here than the claim to absolute divinity.

B. And John's Gentile readers would be no less aware of it than would the Jewish audience. Much in John's gospel reflects clear knowledge of contemporary heathen thought and of current pagan terms. The Egyptian deity, Anubis, Attis of Asia Minor, Marduk of the Babylonians and the Phrygian Baal, were all called shepherds, and so was Zarathustra, founder of the Persian religion, and, among other legendary Greek heroes, Agamemnon. John's insistence that Jesus is the true Shepherd side-glances deliberately at such claims, and underlines once again the whole thesis of his gospel, the everlasting, absolutely unique, divine sonship of Jesus.

III. The measureless offer of ministry

As always in the New Testament, the breathtaking theological claim and declaration are not made for their own sake, but as foundations for affirming what Christ will do for men. Here authority and divinity equip the Shepherd for His manifold ministry to God's flock:

A. *The Good Shepherd seeks:* at considerable trouble (Matthew 12:11), even for one out of a hundred (Luke 15:4), and until he finds it (Luke 15:5). Both Ezekiel (34:11, 12) and Psalm 23 (verse 3a) declare this to be the sure mark of the real shepherd — "He restores my soul." And not because the sheep are attractive, or pitiful, but because He counts them *valuable.*

B. *The Good Shepherd gathers:* the sheep know their shepherd's voice (John 10:3, 5) even as the blind man knew the voice (only) of the One who had healed him (John 9:36, 37). That same Voice shall gather "the lost sheep of the house of Israel," and beyond Israel — the "other sheep" of John 10:16. So shall God's flock be no longer as sheep without a shepherd, scattered, leaderless, but one flock, under one Shepherd.

C. *The Good Shepherd cares:* the green pastures and still waters of Psalm 23 and the exquisite attentiveness of the sheep's every need required in Ezekiel 34:4 are underwritten and guaranteed in John 10:9 — "If any one enters by me, he will be saved, and will go in and out and find pasture."

D. *The Good Shepherd defends:* shepherding was a dangerous trade: Jacob complains of heat and frost, David of wild beasts, Jesus mentions wolves, thieves, and violent robbers (Genesis 31:40; I Samuel 17:34-36; John 10:12, 8; and Matthew 26:31). The sheep being imperiled, the Good Shepherd draws their danger upon Himself, giving His life for their safety. The wolves of sin and death devour Him, not us: He lives to guard us, and dies for our defense.

E. *The Good Shepherd folds,* forever, in the final security of heaven, the whole flock of God. He comes that the sheep might have life, and none can pluck them from His hand. He loses none, and "they shall never perish." "He leads them unto living fountains of water" in the eternal fold (Revelation 7:15-17), and they dwell in the house of the Lord for ever.

Measureless ministry indeed!

Conclusion

> *"He saves the sheep, the goats He doth not save!"* ...
> *So spake the fierce Tertullian. But she sighed,*
> *The infant Church! Of love she felt the tide*
> *Stream on her from her Lord's yet recent grave.*
> *And then she smiled; and in the Catacombs* ...
> *On those walls subterranean, where she hid*
> *Her head 'mid ignominy, death, and tombs,*
> *She her Good Shepherd's hasty image drew —*
> *And on His shoulders not a lamb,* a kid.

(Matthew Arnold)

41. *"I am the Light of the World"*

"I am the light of the world; he who follows me will not walk in darkness but will have the light of life." —John 8:12

Introduction

1. It is easy to be dazzled by words like these — to be so occupied with their poetry, their rhythm, their vast implications, as to miss their immediate, practical meaning. It is certainly a stupendous claim: Jesus declares that He is:

(a) *Universal Light*: not simply light for that age and generation, for that particular society, or as being one element in a whole process of revelation: He is *the* light of the whole world — the light to lighten the Gentiles, the light that illumines every man (Luke 2:32; John 1:9).

(b) *Total Light*: when used by many Gnostics and other pagans, the word "light" meant intellectual illumination, the *knowledge* that they held would save the enlightened. John too contended that Jesus enlightens the darkened mind with the truth that made men free; but for him, as for all Hebrew and Christian thought, "light" means especially moral wisdom, spiritual purity, divine glory. God Himself is light — perfect, radiant, unshadowed holiness (I John 1:5f; James 1:17). So Jesus is claiming to be light to the whole man, not just to the mind: light for mind and conscience and spirit and heart and society.

(c) *Personal Light*: "*I* am the light . . ." — not the teaching or the example but Himself. It lies not in ideas but in fellowship, not in thinking but in following. *He* is the world's illumination, the master light of all our seeing, without whom all life remains a dark enigma and a menacing mystery. He that has the Son has light, as well as life.

2. Such are the wide implications of these glorious words: yet the practical meanings of the claim demand most attention. We shall find them underlined as we watch the occasions when Jesus spoke thus of Himself.

I. At the Feast of Tabernacles

A. This was a joyous festival combining the themes of Harvest and the Exodus story, eight happy days of song and story and sacred celebration. At one point in the ritual, a procession of priests carried — with singing — jars of water from the well at Siloam and with appropriate words and praise poured it out within the Temple precincts, recalling the water that gushed from the rock for Israel in the wilderness, and giving thanks for God's precious gift for man and beast. Throughout the ceremonial the great candelabra, fed by bowls of oil, blazed with light recalling the "pillar of fire": an ancient description declares "there was not a courtyard in Jerusalem that did not reflect the light . . . men of piety used to dance before the illuminations with burning torches in their hands, singing . . ." (Sukka 5:2-4). Meanwhile Israel went camping — dwelling for the festival in tents and booths in memory of the wilderness wandering.

B. John 7:37-38 shows Jesus using the water-ritual as a dramatic "visual aid" to symbolize His claim to be the water of life to thirsty souls. John 8:12 — almost certainly on the same occasion (see RSV) — shows Jesus using the "pillar of fire" ritual as an equally dramatic illustration of His claim to be the light of the world. It needs little imagination to realize the profound impression Jesus' public interruption of the Feast would cause, and the animated discussion His interpretation of the ancient story would arouse.

C. The point of the great claim here, therefore, is that Jesus is the Christian's pillar of fire for his journey through the desert and the darkness of the world. The world is our wilderness: and so often its wisdom, standards, traditions, and culture are darkened and astray — except

122

for Christ. He is *the light that guides* — as the huge Pharos lighthouse at Alexandria (built 300 B.C.) was said to guide ships safely into harbor from 60 miles out at sea; as a "city set upon a hill" with house-lights, fires, and watchman's flares, guided the late traveler overtaken by the darkness; as a leader with a shaded torch might guide some secret party to a night attack, and "he that followeth" closely shall not walk in darkness nor into fatal danger. Jesus, Light of the world, is the light we follow, guiding home across the wilderness where all other landmarks lie hidden, and the marsh lights betray. He is our pillar of cloud by day and of fire by night.

II. At the healing of a man born blind

A. The connection of darkness with physical blindness, and of light with healing of the blind, is emphasized repeatedly in John (9:2-5, 39-41; 11:9-10). Questioned by the disciples about a man born blind, the Master replies, "As long as I am in the world, I am the light of the world." Here the need arises, not from the dark wilderness of the objective world, but from the subjective inability to see, to appreciate, or even to discern, what light nature, experience, conscience, or revelation might provide. To illumine the situation is not enough if men are blind; the Light of the world must open men's eyes.

B. What this spiritual blindness actually means in life may be gathered from scattered Scripture references to this theme:

> *The blind man, in his darkness, hides his sin,* and will not come to the light, that it might be exposed, nor confess it, that it might be cleansed (John 3:19-21; I John 1:6-10).

> *The blind man, in his darkness, stumbles on his way,* giving offence to others, and stumbling into sin; he falls through ignorance, unwariness, a darkened conscience, as well as through willfulness (John 11:9, 10; I John 2:10).

> *The blind man, in his darkness, cannot do God service,* for he does not know what God's work is, nor what God requires; the blind heart blunders, even when it means well (John 9:4).

> *The blind man, in his darkness, wanders without aim;* he drifts without direction, compass, or goal; "he knows not where he goes" (John 12:35; I John 2:11).

Jesus, the Light of the world, is the answer to this fourfold blindness: He exposes sin in order to forgive it; He enlightens the stumbling in order to uphold them; He directs the heart in service, and gives to all life's effort and hope a clear aim and direction. He is the light of the blind — of everyman.

III. At the hour of His own rejection

The great claim is repeated yet a third time (John 12:35-36, 46-48; 11:8-10, with 9:4). Here two ideas are implied:

A. *While the worker has light, he is invulnerable.* God's "day" is for him an appointed time; while it lasts, no one can touch him. When the disciples remonstrate with Jesus for returning into hostile Jewry, He replies, "Are there not twelve hours in the day?" When others warn Him about the hostility of Herod, Jesus makes a similar reply: He has today, and tomorrow; the third day will see His work done— then (and only then) Herod may get his chance (Luke 13:31-32). And so, the work almost done, when the officials come to arrest Jesus He can say, "This is your hour . . ." (Luke 22:53). Always Jesus Himself possesses this sense of His life's day ordered by God's hand, His soul immune until His work is done. And to walk in His light is to share that assurance: it is to walk in safety and to work with high courage, unafraid.

B. *While the world has light, it must decide.* This thought also is in the third assertion of Jesus' claim. He is the Light of the world . . . while He is here (John 9:5). But the light will be withdrawn. It is here "a little longer. . . . Believe while you may . . . lest darkness overtake you" (John 12:35-36). These verses, and indeed the whole of the closing chapters of John, are full of the impending death of Jesus, the judgment of Satan, the judgment of the world: all point to the absolute necessity of decision — soon, and finally, and aright. The condemnation will be that light has come, but men love darkness rather than light (John 3:19). If we cannot find salvation while the light shines, how shall we fare in the darkness? If we will not decide in the day, shall the night find us safe?

Conclusion

The response to Christ's superb claim and invitation is very simple:

Come to the light, with penitence, confession, faith, that sin may be dealt with (John 3:19-21).

Believe on the light, so as to follow implicitly wherever He leads (John 12:36, 44, 46).

Walk in the light, keeping your life transparently under God's judgment (John 12:35; I John 1:6, 7).

Reflect the light, for we also are the light of the world: lives possessing "the Light of the world" should surely be radiant! (Matthew 5:14).

> *Light of the world, for ever, ever shining,*
> *There is no change in Thee;*
> *True light of life, all joy and health enshrining,*
> *Thou canst not fade or flee.*

> *Thou hast arisen, but Thou declinest never;*
> *Today shines as the past;*
> *All that Thou wast Thou art, and shalt be ever,*
> *Brightness from first to last.*

Night visits not Thy sky, nor storm, nor sadness;
Day fills up all its blue,
Unfailing beauty and unfaltering gladness,
And love for ever new.

Light of the world, undimming and unsetting,
O shine each mist away!
Banish the fear, the falsehood, and the fretting;
Be our unchanging day.

(Horatius Bonar)

42. *"I am the Door"*

Young People's Sermon

"I am the door: if any one enters by me, he will be saved, and will go in and out and find pasture." —John 10:9

Introduction

1. Do you remember that great stone door, heavy and solid and immovable, without a handle or a lock, that yielded only to the magic words "Open Sesame!" — and led into the richest cave in all the world? Do you remember the secret door, along the dark corridor, and down the twisting stairs, that opened only if you found the right berry in the old oak carving and pressed your foot at the same time against the panelling — the door that led to mystery and danger and wonderful adventure in forgotten secret rooms? Do you remember that other door, so little that no one noticed or remembered it was there, overgrown with weeds and rusted on its hinges — in the high grim wall, too smooth to climb, too high to leap, too strong to break down — the wall that imprisoned the beautiful princess until Prince Charming patiently and unfalteringly examined every inch of every stone in every stretch of masonry, until he found the long-forgotten door. And how it opened at a touch! And they lived happily ever after! For that matter, do you remember the low door in the wide overshadowing tree, that let Alice into wonderland?

2. The storytellers seem very fond of doors: narrow and rusted and secret and concealed, or high and imposing and invitingly open. Doors that lead to treasure and to beauty, to adventure and to happiness. Why, I wonder, — are all the story-tellers carpenters, who want to advertize their trade? Or is it because the stories are for *young* people, and youth is the time of opening doors — all around you? Doors of

125

learning and door of friendship, doors of great ambitions and high hopes, doors of the wide world and all the years to be: doors of love and work, of marriage and career, of freedom and of faith. The story-tellers know: behind every door is excitement, opportunity, something new to be explored and won. And Jesus said: "I am the Door."

3. We usually put it the other way round: we see Christ standing at the door, begging admission. Holman Hunt painted Him so — bearing His lantern through the gloom to the threshold of our hearts, a threshold overgrown with brambles, weeds and creepers, and there gently knocking with scarred hand, pleading to come in. But the latch is on the inside. He is the Suppliant, the Caller: ours the fast-barred door. Yet that is only *half* the truth. The other half is this: that we stand on His threshold — we are the knockers, the suppliants; He is the Door, bearer of the keys, of David, of death, of Hades, and of life too. He is the Door to adventure and beauty, to freedom and joy: His name the "Open Sesame!" to incalculable good.

4. And it is not so childish an idea, either. For this is the new phrase in much present-day discussion about the world — the jargon of the talkative johnnies: is this an open or a closed universe? *Closed!* say some of the scientists, the logicians, the men of theories and statistics and law and necessity; all moves inevitably, they say, unalterably forward in a closed circle of self-acting forces and self-operating law in a predetermined sequence. There is no freedom: nothing revolutionary or voluntary or really human. *All the doors are closed.* No! shout the heroes, the pioneers, the artists and the thinkers, the leaders and the saints: the world is not shut: men may refuse, rebel, reject, respond, in the sovereign freedom of unfettered responsibility. The future is man's to make, not supinely to wait for; human personality stands at the open doors of life, able to go anywhere until its own choices narrow the alternatives. And Jesus stands with these, challenging the dark and dismal view of a world closed, hopeless, shuttered and narrow. "I am the Door," He proclaims, the open door to every possibility of spiritual adventure, of freedom and enrichment and enlargement. He announces, in the synagogue at Nazareth, the opening of the prison-house; He offers Himself to men as the way out, the way forward, and the way up. He is the open Door.

Think what He promises:

I. Jesus, the Door to new life

A. All kinds of happenings can shut doors to us: failure, disappointment, our own wrong decisions, tragedy. Even these, faced out honestly in the spirit and faith of Jesus, may prove to be only half-shut — or sometimes we find another has opened beside them, leading to unexpected opportunity. But nothing shuts doors so swiftly, so conclusively, as sin. Every evil choice slams the door to some fine opportunity, some anticipated good: and when evil choices have become a habit we find indeed that our world has closed against us, shuttered, and forbidding; and within our own nature the doors of spiritual hope stand shut, for we are what we have made ourselves, and the fetters on our freedom are those our own willfulness has forged. Shut within the prison of a sinful nature, what can we do? "Can the leopard change his spots?" "Can a man begin again when he has grown old in sin?"

B. Putting the question that way, we immediately remember Jesus sitting face to face with an old man. He was not outwardly a man bound in sin; but he was bound and fettered all the same — bound to the past of Judaism, bound to the old, disappointing order, with a legalistic mind and a shell-backed soul; he had no confidence in new truth, no place for young new prophets, no anticipation of new and transfiguring experiences. He had grown old in disappointment, as so many do. And he felt, and said wistfully, that it was impossible now to change, impossible to go back, to begin again. And Jesus said to this old man: "What you need is to be born again!" Precisely that: to be born from above, to begin again on a new level, with new resources and new life; to start afresh in the kingdom not of the flesh but of the free-blowing, unfettered Spirit. Christ opened a door to Nicodemus: the door to new life.

C. For life is never hopeless, given Christ. If any man come to be in Christ, he is a new creation: all things are for him made new. When sin has slammed shut all the doors of hope, Jesus opens new ones: we become as little children, standing again at God's thresholds. Even young people, to whom disappointment can be so bitter, so overwhelming, need His ever open door of life.

II. Jesus, the Door to abundant life

A. But to what kind of life does Jesus introduce us? Our text gives a plain answer! It comes, you will remember, in the middle of the Good Shepherd passage, where Jesus is comforting a man, once blind but now healed, whom the Pharisees have "cast out" of the fold of Judaism, because he defended Jesus. Jesus replies that He — not the self-appointed Pharisees — is the divine, the true Shepherd of God's fold: He alone can bid men enter, or cast them out. Indeed He is Himself the Door: if any man seeks to enter the fold by any other way, he is a thief, a robber, taking what does not belong to him. But those who enter by Jesus, the true Door, find what they seek, and what shall certainly be theirs: abundant life.

B. And what *that* means, Jesus immediately explains. "If any one enters by me . . ."

1. ". . . *he will be saved*" — that is, he will find *safety*. Outside are the thieves, the wolves, and the wilderness, the wild hills with precipices and thorns that trap the unwary sheep. Life is dangerous, and

the way treacherous. But with his heart and mind safe within the fold of God, he can face the dangers, the temptations, the fears, with courage and strength. He cannot avoid the struggle and the conflct; but he can go to it prepared, a life of purity and power so filling and overflowing his soul that the lure of the world has no power over him. Beset with wolves, he is inwardly safe, within the fold of God.

2. "... *he shall go in and out*" — not needing to cower from his enemies, or shrink from the world in cowardly fear of lovely things, in negative, unnatural, unlovely rejection of every beautiful, joyous thing that God has given us: that is a new bondage, not freedom. But he who enters by Christ, the Door, into abundant life, finds *liberty*. Inward victory sets him free to come in and go out, unafraid. He will not play with sin, nor dally with temptation: but he will live in the freedom that only they know whose hearts are bound fast to Jesus, in love and loyalty and joy.

3. "... *and find pasture.*" — Christ's sheep are contented: they lie down in green fields and are led beside still waters. Those who enter Christ's door find all-*sufficiency*: they are satisfied. Abundant life is full of enjoyment, gladness, and deep contentment. It wants nothing, because it overflows.

That is the life into which Jesus ushers us: safety, liberty, sufficiency — and all in abundant measure!

III. Jesus, the Door to everlasting life

A. We need not linger over this, because young people are not usually very concerned about immortality. Yet we remember it was a *young* man, rich, and admired, and in authority, who came running down the road and through the crowd to kneel at Jesus' feet and ask the way to everlasting life. Perhaps young people do see beyond the ends of their noses: do see, as clearly as anyone else, that if men die like dogs and rot like trees, then nothing is really worth while: all temptation and struggle and patience and suffering, all toil and achievement and heroism and saintliness come to nothing in the end — unless man lives for ever. Life is after all a prison, and death its warden . . . and all the doors may as well stay shut if the last door is locked and bolted forever against us.

B. But Jesus denies that. He is the Door to everlasting life — the life abundant overflows earth and time and the present life, and stretches forward. "He that liveth and believeth in me shall never die"; "I give them eternal life, and they shall never perish"; "I have the keys of death, and hell" (John 10:28-30; Revelation 1:18). Life's perspective stretches endlessly ahead, setting all present experience in its true light, because the Door He opens shall nevermore be shut.

C. This is the meaning, of course, of all those open doors of Easter Day: the door of the tomb in the garden stood open, the stone rolled away;

the door of the Upper Room, bolted and barred against the Jews, stood open for Him; the doors of the truth of God were wide for Him and for them to whom He opened up the scriptures; and as He sent them forth into all the world, the doors of the future stood wide for His men. All doors are useless where the risen Jesus walks: because He is Himself the Door to everlasting life.

Conclusion

All this is true of course because Jesus is the open door to God: "No man comes to the Father but by me," He said; and Paul answers, "Through Him we have access . . . to the Father" (John 14:6; Ephesians 2:18). Yet — mark this well — a door is only an *opportunity*. To admire it is not to enter it. We may stand before the magic cave for years, we may whisper about the secret door upon the stair for the rest of our lives. We may gaze on Alice's tree, and watch the brambles thicken over the high, grim wall — and it shall profit us nothing. The treasure, the adventure, the wonder and the joy are for those who enter. Jesus beckons us to LIFE. We must rise, and enter, and explore, if we would live.

43. "I am the True Vine"

"I am the true vine, and my Father is the vinedresser." —John 15:1

Introduction

What, then, was the vine that was *not* true? Each great claim of Jesus in John's gospel implies a direct comparison with other claimants. When Jesus names Himself "the true and living Way," the contrast intended is with the Judaistic "way" of legalism. He is the "true Bread from heaven" in contrast with the manna which Moses provided, and "the good Shepherd" as compared with the false, self-appointed shepherds of Judaism. Immediately therefore we look for the contrast between the "true Vine" and some other false or barren vine — and at once the whole passage becomes sharper, more challenging, and even more compelling.

I. The false vine and the faithless husbandmen

A. No Jew would fail to understand our Lord's use of the vine theme. In a favorite scripture passage, Isaiah had glowingly described how God chose Canaan as His vineyard and transplanted Israel with His own hands from Egypt, giving to the tender plant every possible attention and every advantage of soil and shelter. Isaiah 5:1-7 dwells upon the details of God's election and preparation of Israel to be His fruitful vine. But when the time for grapes had come, God was deeply disappointed — the fruit was sour and useless: injustice, violence and oppression of the helpless and the poor were all the fruit Israel bore for Him. Though the prophet's strictures were sharp, the implied divine favor and purpose remained a welcome theme for Jewish thought.

B. Jeremiah echoes the idea: "I planted you a choice vine, wholly of pure seed; how then have you turned degenerate and become a wild vine?" (2:21). So does Hosea: "Israel is a luxuriant vine that yields its fruit" — this might have been the text upon which Isaiah elaborated! Ezekiel too uses the figures of the vine to prophesy concerning Israel's transplanting into exile (Ezekiel 17:1-10). And Psalm 80:8-16 expresses well the consternation of a later generation at the invasion of God's vineyard by plundering marauders. There is no doubt therefore that our Master's words struck echoes in every hearer's heart. If the scriptures were unfamiliar, then the great golden vine that overspread the "great door of the house" in the Temple would call to mind the fundamental thought — that Israel was God's vine, destined to bear fruit to God in all the earth. And if even the Temple were unfamiliar, then the use of the vine leaf on Jewish coins would still keep the idea in mind.

C. Jesus therefore often set His message against this background of thought:

> in the parable of the laborers in the vineyard, discontented with their reward (Matthew 20:1-16)
> in the parable of the wicked vinedressers, who withheld the proceeds of the vineyard from God their overlord (Luke 20:9-16)
> in the frequent reminders that the quality of the fruit is the only proof of the quality of the tree (Matthew 7:16-20 and elsewhere)
> in the repeated references to the sin of barrenness — in spoken parable (Luke 13:6-9) and acted parable-sign (Mark 11:12-14, 20-21)

and here yet again, in the discourse of the Upper Room, the vine of Israel is in His mind, and the disappointment of God. For God has a *right* to fruit — the right of creation, of election and of great favor shown to Israel. The fruit expected was a holy, righteous national life, and leadership and witness among the nations: instead Judaism had proved a barren tree — fit only to be cut down, cursed, handed over to others. The old vine had been found worthless, and must be destroyed. For the vine is otherwise useless: "Is wood taken from it to make anything? Do men take a peg from it to hang any vessel on? . . . can it ever be used for anything!" (Ezekiel 15:2-5). Fruit alone creates its value: that missing, destruction must follow.

II. The True Vine and the fruitful branches

A. Yet God, the patient Vinedresser, still desires a fruitful vine within the earth. He has planted Jesus — the True Vine — to replace Israel; and with Him are joined other branches, by discipleship and faith, in an organic unity of life. *This* Vine and its branches are not constituted — as Israel was — upon inheritance and blood relationship and national unity, but upon a living unity, a fruitful sharing of divine life with the main Stem — Jesus. This is the grandeur, and the immensity, of the claim: Jesus and His own supplant the vine of Israel. Rooted in Palestine, the branches of the New Vine over-run the earth; planted in the first century, they stretch to the end of time.

B. But this Vine, too, *must* bear fruit to God. What is at stake is the fruitfulness of Christ's whole ministry. Already one apparent branch has broken away, fruitless and diseased — Judas has withstood the sharing of Christ's inner life and has closed his heart against Jesus, and the moment of the outward break has now arrived. The fruitless branch must go: indeed only by bearing fruit do we prove that we *are* branches (John 15:8). And to bear fruit requires only that we "abide in Him" (15:5).

C. Both the severance of the fruitless and abiding of the fruitful are relentlessly analyzed in this exquisite passage. *Severance*: first comes the hidden cracking of the branch from the main stem — some inner disloyalty, prayerlessness, harbored sin (he "does not abide" 15:6). Then comes the more obvious breaking away, as the fibres shrivel and the weight bears the branch down: Christian devotion, worship, fellowship, and work begin to decay, and the breach is made public. Then comes final separation, the gathering of the dead wood for burning: "they" gather them, for even men have no use for fruitless Christians! Yet alongside this spiritual declension there proceeds a divine pruning by the Vinedresser Himself (15:2), as truth begins to offend the faithless soul, and exhortation is resisted, and grace refused. We think we "resign": in fact the Husbandman has pruned us away. The severance of the heart from the source of life in Christ leads thus inevitably to fruitlessness, withering and death. Without Him we are all dry sticks.

D. *Abiding*, too, is explained by detailed analysis: it means quite simply *remaining* in Christ, the heart ever open Christwards. But what a rich inner fellowship that implies!

> *"My words abide in you"* suggests a treasuring and exploring all that He has said, and still says, to us; and it means also keeping His commandments, by a habit of continual obedience (verse 10) — else *knowing* His words will prove utterly profitless. This is *the abiding of the will* in Christ, in faithful obedience and surrender. And one mighty blessing of the surrendered heart is

specially named: it can ask what it wills and is sure of receiving what it asks — for it cannot ask outside of God's will!

"Abide in my love" suggests keeping our hearts within the circle of His felt love and care. He has loved us (verse 9): this we know by every word of the gospel: but sometimes anxieties, disobedience, mistrust, or simple carelessness cloud that love for us. Sometimes, too, we lose the sense of His love for us because we fall "out of love" with our brethren (verse 12). To remain where His love placed us — sure of it, delighting in it — that is *the abiding of the heart,* in trust and peace.

"My joy in you . . . your joy may be full" suggests the continual happiness of a soul that never strays from the source of all joy. It is *the abiding of the whole spirit* in enjoyment of Jesus, that neither doubt nor disloyalty is allowed to spoil.

These are simple Christian counsels, yet they add up to an adhering, a clinging, to Christ, mentally, emotionally, prayerfully, obediently, in fellowship with others, that insures continual spiritual nourishment, and therefore continual and lasting fruit (verse 4), much fruit (verse 5), and still more fruit (verse 2): the fruit of holiness, character, witness and work.

Conclusion

The whole conception of the new Vine of God, and the demand for fruitfulness, may leave us breathless, even perhaps a little discouraged. The ideal is so high! Yet notice where it all begins: "I have loved you . . . You are my friends . . . I chose you and appointed you . . . I have spoken to you that my joy may be in you . . . Herein is my Father glorified. . . ." All the initiative is with God, the Vinedresser, who wills our fruitfulness. There is no need, and no excuse, for severance. We have only to cling to Christ . . . and the fruit will come.

44. *"I am the Resurrection and the Life"*

"I am the resurrection and the life; he who believes in me, though he die, yet shall he live, and whoever lives and believes in me shall never die." —John 11:25, 26

Introduction

1. This is an unpreachable text, and this cannot be a sermon in the usual meaning of the word. Some scripture passages are so breathtaking, daring, final, that the earnest mind can only listen and wonder,

meditate and worship. Explanation, exposition, and application simply fail. And this claim of Jesus is among the very greatest of such utterances. It must be either the simple truth or the utmost of arrogant stupidity. Yet, from another point of view, it is obvious. If Christ be all He claimed, and all that Christians believe, this culmination of His saving power is logically inevitable. All else that His redemption promises would fail, if death be not conquered.

2. The whole ministry of Jesus illustrates this. Christ being once present within suffering humanity, conflict with all that spoils and imperils man's life followed automatically — conflicts with sickness, madness, leprosy, demons, hunger, affliction, sin. At every point the Kingdom He enshrined, the love and power that He embodied, were triumphant: the whole kingdom of evil recoiled from Him, defeated. Could death be the exception — the point of Christ's defeat? Far from it: the gospels show clearly His advancing victory —

> He healed, at a touch, one whose life was draining away, the woman in the crowd (Mark 5:25-34).
> He healed, with a word, one whose life was long paralyzed, truly a living death (Mark 2:3-12).
> He healed, with a gracious call, one whose life had so recently ebbed that death was disputable — the daughter of Jairus (Mark 5:35-43).
> He healed, with a command, one who was being carried to his burial (Luke 7:11-15); and so, supremely.
> He healed, with imperious challenge, one who had lain four days within the tomb (John 11).

Dare we draw a line to His all-conquering power?

3. And everything about this final demonstration of His might lends added drama to the deed. It happens almost underneath Jerusalem's walls, on the brink of His final challenge to the nation. It forms a glorious rehearsal for His own Easter triumph, coming now so soon. All the circumstances make the story unforgettable: our Lord's deep personal affection for this household; His own peril (11:8, 16); His deep "groaning" sympathy; the sisters' quiet challenge ("Lord, if you had been here . . .") and His gentle reply; His earnest prayer; the astonished bystanders; the enraged authorities; and the underlying suggestion that all was deliberate, stage-managed, calculated, as prelude to that last week of challenge and decision. Here is a story that, *in its place in history,* has immeasurable significance. But we read it now as the appropriate setting for these unsurpassable words:

> "I am the resurrection and the life; he who believes in me, though he die, yet shall he live, and whoever lives and believes in me shall never die."

Allowing, then, the glorious affirmation to make its own impact on meditative minds, let us note first how:

133

I. Jesus drags the whole concept of immortality out of the future and into the present.

A. Offering to Martha in her bereavement the comfort of a great hope, Jesus says, "Your brother shall rise again." He receives the reply, "I know he will . . . at the last day." And He answers *in the present tense,* "I am the resurrection. . . ." Some Jews, it is true, had reached a *doctrine* of eternal life, an ultimate hope, a logical inference concerning God and His covenant with men. But Jesus makes that hope an experiential reality. The conquest of death, resurrection, eternal life, — all is there, our Lord declares, there and present, now, in Him. With us already is the risen Christ: in Him we *live.*

B. This daring thought is basic to John's whole teaching on salvation as eternal life. Always the tense is present: the assurance is ours here and now. "God has given us eternal life, and this life is in His Son; we know that we have eternal life; he who believes in the Son has eternal life; he who hears and believes has eternal life — has passed from death to life (I John 5:11-13; John 3:36; 5:24). In Christ we are already immortal!

C. Paul is equally emphatic that eternal life is ours, now, in Christ. We were dead in trespasses and sins, but have been made alive in Christ, planted together in the likeness of His resurrection, risen with Christ, enjoying the gift of God which is eternal life. We ought therefore to live as those "on the other side of death," as heirs of God and fellow heirs with Christ, the life of Jesus being already manifest in our body. Some, he says, may pass through death, others will be "changed," but alike we prove already the power of His resurrection, and possess already His victorious life in us.

D. All this is no mere vivid metaphor. Though physical death confronts us, life continues through death unbroken. This is apostolic teaching — that we now possess life eternal; it is apostolic exhortation, that we live uncrushed by sorrow, undefeated by fear . . . *immortally unafraid.*

II. Jesus, in consequence, robs death of all ultimate reality.

A. "He who believes in me, though he die, yet shall he live, and whoever lives and believes in me shall never die." The words startle us by their incredible assurance. Physical change and separation are certain: but not *death,* not the destruction of the self, not the loss of identity, or of values, or of knowledge, or of relationships, or of love. Death, the last enemy, being under His feet, ceases to be an enemy. A Puritan classic bears the challenging title "The Death of Death in the Death of Christ"; one of the most widely known and often sung hymns of the Western Church calls Jesus "Death of death and Hell's destruction."

B. Part of the meaning of this transfiguration of death lies in the apt and eloquent new name Christians gave to it: Stephen "fell asleep";

Jairus' daughter "is not dead but sleepeth"; "our friend has fallen asleep," says Jesus of Lazarus, "I go·to awake him out of sleep." In the Christian catacombs beneath the city of Rome, the frequent inscription meets us, "Goodnight — the morning comes!" In such language death has lost its *finality*: death has no more dominion — it becomes sleep in prospect of morning:

> . . . . *we fall to rise,*
> *Are baffled to fight better,*
> *Sleep to wake.*

C. But the rest of the meaning of Christ's transfiguration of death lies in the fact that the dead "sleep" because they never really died —

> *O lord of life, where'er they be*
> *Safe in Thine own eternity*
> *Our dead are living unto Thee —*
> *Hallelujah!*

Death has lost its *reality,* too. "There is no death" cries Longfellow, "what seems so is transition";

> *"There is no death! the stars go down*
> *To rise upon some other shore,*
> *And bright in heaven's jewelled crown*
> *They shine for ever more."*

sang J. L. McCreery. While from the death-cell of a Nazi prison at Plotzensee, a young German woman (aged 23) condemned to die for two months' membership of a political group, wrote in February, 1943:

In the first few days after the verdict I was in a most extraordinary mood. I was completely ready to die — for what, I really did not know — but death itself did not seem horrible to me and does not now. *There is no death* — that I am absolutely sure of.

D. This is the faith that calls death's bluff, that knows that they who depart are "with Christ . . . far better."

> *And life for them is life indeed,*
> *The splendid goal of life's strait race,*
> *And where no shadows intervene*
> *They see Thy face.*

> *Not as we knew them any more,*
> *Toilworn, and sad, with burdened care —*
> *Erect, clear-eyed, upon their brows*
> *Thy name they bear.*

> *Free from the fret of mortal years,*
> *And knowing now Thy perfect will,*
> *With quickened sense and heightened joy*
> *They serve Thee still.*

> *O fuller, sweeter is that life,*
> *And larger, ampler is the air:*
> *Eye cannot see nor heart conceive*
> *The glory there:*
>
> *Nor know to what high purpose Thou*
> *Dost yet employ their ripened powers,*
> *Nor how at Thy behest they touch*
> *This life of ours.*
>
> *There are no tears within their eyes,*
> *With love they keep perpetual tryst;*
> *And praise and work and rest are one*
> *With Thee, O Christ.*
>
> (W. C. Piggott)

To glowing confidence like that, death has lost all reality.

III. And Jesus does all this to death, because He is Himself the life.

A. "I am the resurrection **and the life**" — the additional words are vital to the truth. Eternal life possessed now, death transfigured and ended, might be little more than words, ideas, doctrines, unless already we possess "Christ our life" (Colossians 3:4). The reality of Christian hope depends entirely on the depth of Christian life. This finds beautiful illustration in the story before us. For the basis of this stupendous miracle was the friendship of Lazarus and Jesus. This was a home where Jesus was deeply, devotedly loved (verses 3, 5, 11, 33, 35, 36, and 38 underline the point!). *And divine friendships are not broken.*

B. This is the oldest of all arguments for immortality. God deigns to share this life with His children, and cannot lightly consent to let them go. So the Psalmist in Psalm 16:5-11 recites what God is to him now — a chosen portion, who gives counsel, and instruction, who is always before me, and at my right hand — and then argues, "My body also dwells secure, For thou dost not give me up to Sheol, or let thy godly one see the Pit." The argument reappears in Psalm 73:23-26 — "I am continually with Thee, Thou dost hold my right hand; Thou dost guide me with Thy counsel and afterward Thou wilt receive to glory. Whom have I . . . but Thee. . . . God is the strength of my heart and my portion for ever." And it recurs yet again in Psalm 139: the God who has searched me and known me, all my ways, besetting me behind and before and laying His hand upon me — whither shall I flee from His Spirit? "In heaven, or in Sheol, Thou art there. . . ." Always the present experience of God's fellowship is the basis of hope for future life. *Divine friendships are not broken*: to walk with God is to find "translation," for God will not consent to lose His own.

C. And this is Christ's argument. "He is not the God of the dead but of the living, for all live unto Him." The homes where He is loved shall find their circle at last complete. The friendship forged in faith shall be strong still in death and shine in eternity. Those who know themselves to be in Christ called and justified can already add that they are "glorified" — because they know God's love is stronger than death. *Nothing* — but *nothing* — shall separate us from the love of God in Christ, neither life *nor death*, things present nor things to come. For Christ is our life — now: and shall be an eternal Friend.

"I am the resurrection and the life," saith the Lord; "he who believes in me, though he die, yet shall he live, and whoever lives and believes in me shall never die."

45. *"I ... am He"*

"Jesus said to her, 'I who speak unto you am he.' " —John 4:26

Introduction

1. Among the scenes of Israel's early history which no Jew could ever forget was that described in Exodus 3. Moses stands at the Burning Bush, arguing with God his incapacity to serve God's purpose for Israel, and receiving nevertheless the divine commission to return to Pharaoh and to deliver Israel from bondage. And when Moses pleads that none will listen to him unless he can say who it is that has sent him, he is given — in what many Jews would count one of the most sacred moments in all their long story — the revelation of the most hallowed Name: "God said to Moses, 'I AM WHO I AM.' And he said, 'Say this to the people of Israel, "I AM has sent me to you.' " Whether the correct translation be "I am what I am," or "I will be what I will be" (the name is so brief and elliptical that exact reproduction in English is impossible), the significance is clear: it is the most solemn affirmation of God's changeless, unconditioned, self-sufficient, everlasting existence. He is the One who *is* — period!

2. We can scarcely conceive the sacredness attached to this Name in Jewish minds. The devout held it to be too sacred to pronounce, and never uttered it. The scribes never wrote it out, even in the scriptures: the consonants YHWH were given vowels from another word, meaning "Lord," and so the word was deliberately mispronounced for centuries, till its original sound was actually forgotten. (It passed into English eventually as *Jehovah*.) The superstitious came to treat the unspoken symbol YHWH as a powerful charm, a talisman; Isaiah (47:8) sees the careless use of the word by the idle, luxury-loving rich as sheer

blasphemy. Zephaniah (2:15) regards Nineveh's usurpation of the title — "I am and there is none else" — as the very zenith of pagan godlessness and pride. To Jewish reverence, the word belongs to God alone: He only possesses changeless, self-existent, self-sufficient majesty: He alone can truthfully claim, "I AM."

3. Yet in John's gospel the words are ascribed to Jesus some *fourteen times!*

I. The climax of divine revelation

A. Sometimes, it is true, the great phrase "I am he" — or "I am I" — is simply used for self-identification. In John 9:9 the blind man so uses the words (in Greek) . But even where this is the immediate meaning, when Jesus says "I AM" in 6:20 and in 18:6 and again in 8, the circumstances and the effect lend solemn overtones to the simple words. In the one case He speaks through the storm to frightened hearts of His disciples, and at once they come safely to land; in the other case He is about to be arrested, the disciples start backwards in panic, and as He speaks, "Whom seek ye? . . . I AM He" — police, soldiers, and Judas together are seized with fear and fall backwards to the ground. On His lips, with His accent of authority, the common phrase becomes almost an epiphany!

B. It is impossible, however, to miss in other passages a deliberate echo of the Greek Bible. "I AM the Lord thy God" introduces there the great commandments; "I, I AM he who comforts you" is the message of the great Isaiah for a people bereaved and seemingly desolate (Isaiah 51:12, and again 41:4; 43:10, 13; 46:4; 48:12). In all such passages the solemn affirmation of self-existent Deity is couched in the same Greek words that John ascribes to Jesus, and always with the same suggestion of One forever the same, eternal, unconditioned, self-sufficient. Thus:

in 8:24 unbelief in Christ, the eternal, the One from above, means that men must die in their sins, "unless you believe that I am He";

in 8:28 the divine authority possessed by Christ will one day be surely vindicated, when He has been lifted upon a cross: then "you will know that I am He";

in 8:56-58 Christ claims that Abraham rejoiced to see His day, and underlines the astonishing implication with the explicit statement, "Before Abraham was, I AM"; and

in 13:19 Christ unfolds the future to His disciples, as He who knows the end from the beginning, that when all comes to pass they may know that "I AM HE."

Here, plainly, vast claims are being made; a divine self-consciousness is finding expression in words filled with hallowed associations. Almost certainly, our Lord is echoing the great declaration of God in Isaiah 43:10, 11: "You are my witnesses," says the Lord, "and my servant whom

138

I have chosen, that you may know and believe me that I am He. Before me no god was formed, nor shall there be any after me. I, I am the Lord, and besides me there is no saviour."

C. All this lends exceptional weight to the stupendous affirmations scattered through John's gospel:

I AM the Way, that men should walk
I AM the Bread of life, to sustain for the journey
I AM the Light of the world, that men need not walk in darkness
I AM the Door to ever vaster opportunity and freedom
I AM the Good Shepherd, who guides men safely to God's fold
I AM the True Vine, which shall bear fruit to God
I AM the Resurrection and the Life, that conquers death

Here is a *sevenfold* implication of divinity, and assurance that He can be all this to all men because of Who He is. On other lips the great words would be mockery: from Him they are mercy and salvation.

D. Before such self-revelation the mind can only bow in worship, confessing Him, with Thomas, "My Lord, and my God!" John's gospel is the Christian's Burning Bush: the eternal Christ, the divine I AM speaks from its glowing pages, *breathes in all the colossal claims* John boldly asserts for Jesus, *vindicates all the uncompromising comparisons* with the fruitless vine, the false shepherds, the misleading way, the bread that fails to nourish, and at the same time *justifies the continual concentration* of men's faith and hope upon the Christ. For He is not only the climax of divine revelation, but also . . .

II. The cynosure of human faith and hope

A. Sometimes the great phrase we are studying occurs in special contexts which underline its meaning in ways still closer to our hearts. Thus, its essential meaning appears on the lips of Philip in the excited, glowing testimony to Nathanael — "We have found Him of whom Moses in the law and also the prophets wrote . . ." (John 1:45). In one sentence, all previous religious development through history, law, and prophecy is seen to point forward to Christ, in whom the quest of men like Philip and Nathanael is at last fulfilled. All expectation, hope, and prayer have found their answer; all spiritual longing has found its divine fulfilment; to men whose whole desire, taught by scripture, has been the coming of Messiah, Jesus has at last said in effect, "I am He!" — and they are content.

B. Very similar is the message of Jesus to John the Baptist, sending from prison his wistful question, full of the ardent longing of a faithful prophet whose eyes strain with watching for the Day: "Art Thou He that should come, or look we for another?" (Luke 7:19). Christ's answer is to tell the prophet's messengers to return to John with full reports of the things that they have witnessed, and the word of blessing upon all who shall not stumble at Christ because He is not quite what they expected. The message means clearly, "I am He!" — though you may have to look twice to recognize me!

C. And to the Woman by the well-head, His word is the same. Out of the spiritual thirst that has directed her conversation, and the barren sinfulness of her past life, she has turned aside the directness of Christ's words by raising current questions about where men ought to worship, and rival claims between Samaritan and Jew about religion. The words of Jesus pierce her smoke screen and she perceives He is a prophet: immediately she speaks of the coming of the Christ who will "show us all things" — Who will be the answer to all questions and perplexity, all rivalry and conflict of truth, all spiritual thirst, too, and burdening sin. And to her He says, with gracious finality, "I that speak unto thee am He!" — the complete answer to all her need.

D. When the Greeks come to Jerusalem they ask only to see Jesus; on the Mount of Transfiguration, when the ecstasy is passed, the privileged three awake to see Jesus only. It is natural so; for He is the perfect, final revelation, the ultimate unanswerable answer. Others probe the eternal questions, He resolves them. He puts all straight, clears all doubts, illumines all pressing darkness, and satisfies the mind, the conscience, and the heart. He is the rainbow in whom all pure colors shine, the whole truth in whom all partial truths are comprehended, the sun in whose radiance all other light grows pale, the divine life enshrining all beauty, truth and goodness. "I am He," says Jesus: and our hearts respond with Peter —

Lord, to whom shall we go? You have the words of eternal life; and we have believed, and have come to know, that you are the Holy One of God (John 6:68, 69).

46. Christian Thanksgiving Day

"May you be strengthened with all power, according to his glorious might, for all endurance and patience with joy, giving thanks to the Father, who has qualified us to share in the inheritance of the saints in light. He has delivered us from the dominion of darkness and transferred us to the kingdom of his beloved Son, in whom we have redemption, the forgiveness of sins." —Colossians 1:11-14

Introduction

1. Here is a harmonious quintette of Christian qualities that comprise a balanced, healthy, happy Christian mood — *power* — *endurance* — *patience* — *joy* — *gratitude*. It might well be that in a pagan city like

Colosse, the first and most urgent need of Christian hearts would be for power — to stand for Christ and withstand evil. The first fruit of such inward power is endurance, and the consciousness of strength to endure is the heart of all patience. This, in all circumstances, is the foundation of abiding joy: it is failure and defeat and fear that most often rob us of spiritual happiness. And given such strength to endure with patience, emerging into joy, surely they will be thankful! Paul's prayers are ever thoughtful and informed: if this one is answered, his Colossian converts will be happy Christians.

2. The place of thankfulness here is very significant — the crown and fruit of a balanced life. Yet gratitude can rarely be exhorted or argued into a soul: it is quickened and nourished not so much by a sense of duty as by

> a right appreciation of our privileges
> a vivid realization of how little we deserve
> a keen expectation of constantly unfolding good.

Paul therefore does not argue or plead; instead he states the grounds for Christian gratitude as accepted facts of Christian experience. Rightly valued, they will suffice to sustain a thankful heart.

3. It is tempting to speculate the season of the year when Colossians was written. Certainly, the Passover story of Israel's Exodus from Egypt to Canaan appears to lie behind a number of its phrases. Already the best-known of all stories to a Jewish mind, it provided a scriptural model of Christian experience for gentile converts also. It seems especially to be echoed in Paul's prayer. For the exodus was the migration of a whole people, through *deliverance,* pilgrimage, and conquest, from slavery to freedom, from the *kingdom* of pagan Pharaoh to an *inheritance* in Canaan, the whole event constituting a massive act of divine *redemption.* So the Christian is called, Paul would suggest, to a perpetual Passover of thanksgiving, for a "greater than Moses" has redeemed us, translated us, made us ready for an inheritance among the saints.

I. We owe gratitude for liberation, as Israel did.

A. Christ has endowed life with a new freedom. As surely as was Israel under Moses, we too have been redeemed from fear, from slavery, and from bondage to ourselves. And in the same way — by power and by purchase. The Song of Moses dramatically pictures the astonishment of the neighboring peoples as they watch what God is doing for Israel:

> The peoples have heard, they tremble; pangs have seized on the inhabitants of Philistia.
> Now are the chiefs of Edom dismayed; the leaders of Moab, trembling seizes them;
> All the inhabitants of Canaan have melted away. Terror and dread fall upon them;

Because of the greatness of thy arm they are as still as a stone,
    Till thy people, O lord, pass by
    Till the people pass by whom thou has purchased.

"Thou didst with thine arm redeem thy people," says Psalm 77:15; "I gave Egypt as your ransom, Ethiopia and Seba in exchange for you," replies Isaiah 43:3. Always God redeems by purchase and by power, to set His people free.

B. So at Nazareth, on the threshold of the world's redemption, Jesus proclaimed liberty to the captives, the opening of prisons. It is one of the great keynotes of His gospel: "The Son shall make you free . . . the truth shall make you free . . . ye shall be free indeed." He comes to set men at liberty, to confer the freedom of the sons of God.

> *The essence of this freedom* is "the forgiveness of sins," as Jesus sets men free from past guilt, from burdened conscience, from fear of judgment and from the ultimate consequences of past wrong. There is no bondage like that of the incurable past: no miracle quite so wonderful as that which sets us free to hope again.
> *The result of this freedom* is liberation from the tyranny of tradition, what Peter calls the "vain conversation (manner of living) received by tradition from your fathers"; from the tyranny of rule and ritual, bound upon the conscience by law and fear alone; and from the abject helplessness of a nature spoiled and fettered by past sinfulness — a psychological liberation into the freedom of Christ and the life of His Spirit.

Let us, on every level of experience, "stand fast in the liberty wherewith Christ has set us free"!

C. This gospel of liberation is especially relevant in the modern world, for not only does *modern thought* seem to portray man as imprisoned within a material world of impersonal forces, an instinctive world of animal lusts and limitations, a social world of self-repeating mistakes and self-defeating ideals, a moral world of corruption and despair; in addition, *modern attitudes* appear to take political and religious freedom so much for granted as to endanger both. The twentieth century has good reason to know better — to remember with pain that liberty is fragile, vulnerable, and often betrayed. We do well to keep a Thanksgiving Day for Christian liberation — remembering how Christ broke the power of cancelled sin and set the sinner free, and how by His truth and His Spirit and His love He ushered in a new vision of a free world bound only to what is good and true and lovely. We must remain *grateful for freedom* — lest we lose it.

II. We owe gratitude for translation, too, as Israel did.

A. Christ has transferred life to a new realm. The new freedom of Israel, as she left Egypt, was not to license but to pilgrimage and the discipline of nationhood in Canaan. So the Christian's freedom is neither for chaos nor disorder; it is no free-for-all, do-as-you-please emotional spree: the Christian passes into new allegiance, entirely "under new management."

B. We have been "translated" out of the realm of darkness — from the "Egypt" of our darkened mind and conscience, the bondage of our sin. For the Colossians this meant translation out of the mental and moral world of first-century paganism, deliverance from the besetting fear of a demon-ridden world; for us also it means translation out of the materialism and determinism of our culture, with its sensuality and its selfishness. Unbelievers — in New Testament terms — walk according to the course (the rule of life) of this present world, subjects to ignorance, evil, and death; but those who believe are set free, transported across the Red Sea of baptism (I Corinthians 10:2 suggests this) to another realm, where the tyrannies of sin no longer hold. The old allegiance is cancelled and the old fears are gone.

C. And we have been "translated" into the kingdom of the Son of God's love. It is not yet said to be a kingdom of light — but of love. For the new realm has its law: the rule of love, of Christ the Son of love, a rule gentle though firm, of persuasion and not of power, of grace and gratitude instead of fear. Under His sway, our freedom is kept wholesome and safe and uncorrupting. Here all things are made new to us, all things are now "of God." It becomes the Father's world, and we are citizens of heaven, subjects of a distant (and yet so near) kingdom invisible, in love with another King, whose service is freedom and whose banner over us is love. We do well to keep a Thanksgiving Day for Christian citizenship in the kingdom of the Christ — we shall be better citizens of our nearer homeland if we do!

III. We owe gratitude for expectation, again as Israel did.

A. Christ has illumined life with a new prospect. We have been made *fit* to be partakers of the inheritance of *the saints in light.* Ours is an inheritance of *light,* where evil things that love the darkness cannot live. Therefore it is for saints — all others would be uncomfortable in heaven! So must a man not only be entitled, but *made fit* — to appreciate and to enjoy the things God hath prepared for those that love Him. The "fitness" does not purchase glory — it remains a free inheritance: but by the daily fellowship of Christ, the love of God, and the gentle discipline of the Spirit we are made capable of enjoying the glory that shall be. For the Christian idea of heaven is both pure and purifying.

B. Herein lies the value of the Christian hope of immortality. As Israel's wilderness wandering was lit by the prospect of the land and the life beyond the Jordan, so Christian expectation illumines present experience. It gives increased meaning to today, greater significance to every moral struggle and decision, deeper incentive to every high endeavor. All manhood is ennobled when we declare of any human soul, "he has for ever."

C. That is why it was a turning point in Western culture, not less than in Western Christianity, when Edwin, Anglo-Saxon king of northeast England, considering whether to receive the Christian missionaries, was addressed by one of his noblemen: "The life of man, O King, is like one of your winter feasts. We feed and revel in the great hall about the fire: a sparrow flies in through the archways, out of the storm outside, and while it stays with us feels not the blast and chill. But when the short moment of its happiness and shelter has passed it flies on again into the storm and darkness. Such is the life of man. And if this new faith can give us more of certainty as to what lies beyond, or more of hope, it deserves to be received." So came the Christian expectation and perspective to the hard and ruthless North, redeeming man from the level of the beasts and lifting him to immortal hope. The argument still holds, though modern man likes to pretend he can manage without knowing where he goes!

D. Said a great Christian scholar:
> Christianity has found a new basis for the hope of immortality in the fact of Christ's resurrection;
> and a new centre for it in the personal experience of new life, prophetic of its own immortality;
> we might add, too, that Christianity has found
> a new conception of it in a "Father's house" where the children of the eternal find their inheritance in "light."

We do well to keep Thanksgiving Day for Christian expectation. By our liberation the past is adjusted; by our translation the present is well ordered; by our expectation the future is assured; we have great cause, therefore, to live in gratitude.

47. On Revising One's Hopes

Advent Sunday

"Are you he who is to come, or shall we look for another?" —Luke 7:19

Introduction

1. It is a real victory when the disappointed, puzzled Christian learns to revise his hopes, without losing them, or nursing disillusionment, or becoming cynical. The ability to do so is a sure sign of spiritual maturity. And this is an obvious theme for Advent: for the coming of the Christ was waited for on all hands, yet many expectations had to be reconsidered, many confident forecasts had to be reinterpreted. Jesus fulfilled, and yet disappointed and transformed, so many of the hopes of Israel.

2. John's gospel (7:40-52) illustrates the constant *public* debate that raged round Jesus: the argument and counter-argument, matching prophecies against proof-texts, as men glimpsed, and yet doubted, the fulfillment of Israel's dream. Luke's gospel records the *private* debate that possessed one faithful mind. The Baptist had looked for a Messiah-Judge, with axe, and flail, and fire upon the wicked, but Jesus had come with healing, promise, and gracious invitation. All public and private hopes seemed on the edge of fulfillment — and yet so changed!

3. Israel awaited her Messiah-King, "prince of the house of David," a deliverer like Zerubbabel; another, greater Moses, combined with some heaven-sent angelic Visitant, foreshadowed in apocalyptic. Instead,

> He came a little baby-thing,
> That made a woman cry!

If many were disappointed, some disillusioned, a few grew cynical, yet others revised their hopes, looked again at the divine promises, and saw the hand of God.

4. For God's fulfillments are always greater than His promises. It is a mark of understanding to adjust expectation to God's achievement, to watch Him doing more than we dared to hope. Especially does God love to surprise us in the ways that so startled Jewish hearts, confronted with *Jesus* as the fulfillment of their age-long hopes: — For He proved to be:

I. A far more human figure than they thought

A. *Apocalyptists* foretold a figure from the skies, "Son of Man" on clouds of heaven; supernatural, glorious, frightening.

145

Nationalists awaited a royal figure of power, in all the panoply of authority, military strength, dominion.

Pietists awaited a super-Pharisee, stern, rigorous, of more-than-Moses stature and demand, devoted to Law, a champion of orthodox zeal.

B. He came, a simple Babe, of a peasant family, in ungodly Nazareth! *Moderns* are bothered by *"wonders"* in the story — star, angels, virgin birth: *they* were bothered by *ordinariness* — the human Christ, a spiritual kingdom, in human hearts. He came much nearer to common people, and common need, than they could see! — Yet John declares, "We beheld His glory." God's fulfillments are *always* much nearer home than we expect! We strain our eyes for some exceptional, glorious "far off" event: He unveils His glory on our home-town doorstep.

II. A far more generous figure than they wanted

A. The ancient promises had far *wider* fulfillment than they expected: a Christ for *sinners, Greeks, Romans, the world!* The narrow lineaments of the traditional Messiah would not fit Him: strict definitions broke down when measured against His mind, His ministry, His forecasts, and His love. He was no King for the elect; He served no exclusive national purpose; He offered no limited, concentrated grace. The *Jewish* hope proved to be a blessing for *Gentiles.* He was so much wider than all expectations, or beliefs, that they did not *want* Him.

B. Yet it is always so. God never fulfills a selfish, strictly limited expectation; He never satisfies personal pride, or assists competition against rivals, or bolsters up spiritual snobbery, or confirms us in self-righteousness. Whenever our hopes are circumscribed by self-interest, or nourish exclusiveness, He will break through them. The fulfillment is always larger than our reading of the promise.

III. A far more realistic figure than they expected

A. The Emmaus conversation illustrates this. The sad disciples confess they thought that He would redeem Israel, but His rejection and death have shaken all their confidence. Such a question as "Ought not the Christ to suffer these things . . . ?" would never enter the average Jewish mind: if it did it would receive a short reply — "Of course not!" This was always a difficulty to Jewish minds: the cross became a stumbling-block to men who waited for a *successful* Messiah. But the difficulty began during His ministry: a Messiah who could be weary, contradicted, weeping, criticized, threatened, arrested, was not within their view. Jesus came far nearer human suffering than a "Messiah" would, or could! Not until they — like the two at Emmaus — read their scriptures again, did they understand. Then the question "Ought not . . . ?" received the wondering answer, "But of course . . . !"

B. For where men expected a deliverance *out of* evil and wrong, to be wrought from above, by supernatural means and magic, He brought a deliverance within the evil and the pain, and wrought from within our suffering situation. Before He solved man's problem, He first shared it; before He cleansed our sin, He first bore it on His heart. At this point, most of all, men had to revise their hopes to take in an atoning, vicarious death as part of Messiah's work. In the event, the whole messianic expectation was so radically reinterpreted that men came to speak more often of the Suffering Servant than of the Messiah, and name Jesus Saviour and Redeemer more often than King.

Conclusion

Mature faith must always so revise its hopes, to keep up with God. It is a poor life that does not preserve great dreams and expectations, and work, and wait, and pray for them. But it is a vulnerable, frustrating life that does not learn how often God does great things in unexpected ways; how He fulfills His word to us more humanly, nearer to our common life, through human agencies, than we expected; and more generously, on a wider and less selfish scale; and more realistically, within our situation, where we are, rather than transporting us away.

For Israel's hopes were true, on the whole. It was not a question of making the best of deep disappointment. Jesus was indeed "He that was to come." But He was far greater than all their hopes portrayed. We must often so adjust our hopes, or else stop hoping! Faith must grow to God's fulfilling, and never demand that God conforms to our expecting. God loves to surprise His people!

48. Thy Word Is Like . . . .

Bible Sunday

"So shall my word be." —Isaiah 55:11

Introduction

1. Because the "living" God is revealed in *what He has said* to chosen men, revealing His will, and in *what He has done* among privileged people, revealing His character, the record of His words and deeds becomes itself an operative agency in spiritual experience, a vehicle of spiritual power, the embodiment of saving truth. The Bible is "history preaching" (Forsyth) precisely because it still conveys divine self-revelation to earnest readers: God is *comprehended* and *confronted* in its pages.

2. The everlasting *Word*, within the self-revealing words and deeds, is thus discovered to be a living, fertilizing, awakening, life-conveying principle. This is far better set forth in meaningful metaphors:

I. Thy Word like — rain

A. "As rain . . . snow . . . watereth the earth . . . bring forth and bud . . . seed to sower, bread to eater . . . so shall my word be. . . ." The Prophet sees a whole people trodden by suffering, withered by unbelief, parched, barren, as the Arabian dèsert: a "dry" time, fruitless, joyless; the soul of the people like the baked soil of waterless uplands — till the early and latter rains soften, quicken, burst the buds, break into flower, carpet the earth, until seed, and so bread, spring again. So the *Word* comes refreshingly upon parched souls.

B. A French West Africa missionary, using convalescence as an opportunity to improve his language, was reading his Testament aloud on the veranda: a native gardener carrying water to parched ground repeatedly passed, his steps getting slower each journey, edging nearer, listening — till he was invited to sit and hear: he became the only Christian in that Moslem village.

C. A young Dutch student, Philip de Beaufort, was arrested in 1942, "questioned" by Nazis thirty-six times, and imprisoned over Christmas. A young lad Dirk shared his cell. Beaufort suggested reading aloud "as at home on Christmas eve" — "Now it came to pass in those days there went out a decree from Caesar. . . ." A voice came from the next cell, "Speak up . . ."; "Bring the Bible in here" from another; "Read for us all" called down the corridor: so, standing on a stool near the cell-door grating, in the semi-darkness of a Nazi prison, he read the immortal words. He gave a brief comment, then "Our Father . . ." was taken up in each cell. A hoarse voice began "Silent night, Holy night . . . ," and it was taken up throughout the prison. "It seemed for a moment as if from some deep underlying joy a wave washed over this collection of human misery." Refreshing rain!

II. Thy Word like — seed

A. "The field is the world — the seed is the word of God"; with an extension of meaning — "We are born again of incorruptible seed." — "The word of the truth, the gospel which has come to you, as indeed in the whole world it is *bearing fruit* and *growing*" (Colossians 1:5, 6). So very often the harvest of Christian faith and character springs directly from the Word read or heard.

B. Sometimes the harvest is *slow*, sometimes *swift*:

A Bible colporteur, in Indo-China, eating his supper, asked if the innkeeper was from the far north, because of his accent. The man shyly confessed he was. He could read, had a mission-school background, and knew of Christ, but he had failed to be Christian. After reading and prayer, he found real salvation — years late.

In Africa, a missioner, delayed and stayed overnight with a Roman Catholic native, who, becoming fascinated with the Old Testament story, asked for a Bible. A fortnight later, he turned up at a film show concerning Christ, 40 miles away, with a truckload of friends, who all bought Bibles! Swift harvest of the sacred seed!

III. Thy Word like — mirror

A. James describes a hearer of the word as one observing his natural face in a mirror, noticing, but immediately forgetting, what he was like (1:22-25). Hebrews 11 holds up scriptural examples in which we see ourselves: indeed all things written aforetime were for our learning (Romans 15:4). As we read of David, Peter, Mark, we feel "that's me!" God's self-revealing word reveals also ourselves.

B. A. Singapore contractor, reasonably wealthy, met in a coffeehouse a Christian having copies of the scriptures to sell. For the sake of memories of Sunday school and Church, he agreed to buy, but beat the price down from two-fifty to two dollars. He read all night. The next morning he searched out the Christian to give him the fifty cents, saying, "The Book made me feel *mean*. The Holy Spirit dealt again with my soul as in old days, and brought me back to Christ." The mirror of the word is painfully clear.

IV. Thy Word like — lamp

A. This is probably the most familiar metaphor for scripture: "Thy word is a lamp *unto my feet* . . ." (Psalm 119:105, Proverbs 6:23). It is important, though, to note the terms of the promise — not illumination of all the scenery, all the time, but always light enough to walk by: "for my feet" — all we need!

B. In the Ghana (West Africa) bush, a missionary started, before dawn, in deep mists, upon a 20-mile hike. About halfway he was met by a grinning African boy, bearing the invitation of a nearby Chief, which it would be tactless to ignore. The result was a detour and a long palaver. Then he returned to the track to hasten on his journey. Soon it was the brief twilight, and suddenly dark. The forest on all sides whispered stealthily, the fireflies danced, the track became difficult to follow, and his anxieties multiplied and deepened. Then he heard singing, native hymns, and bursts of laughter, as a group of young men, expecting his arrival, came forward to meet him. Each carried a native lamp, swinging low at his ankles. So together they set forward, by narrowest paths, presently negotiating a precarious tree-trunk bridge across a ravine, the ink-darkness overhead, on each side, before, behind, and beneath, except for the tiny circle, little larger than his foot, from his swinging lamp. "I walked safely," he said, "in illumined pools within the surrounding darkness." At evening prayers, the text *had* to be "Thy word . . . lamp to my feet."

V. Thy Word like — sword

A. In Hebrews 4:12, 13 the word of God is a sword, living, active, piercing, laying bare the secrets of men. In Ephesians 6:17 it is the sword of the Spirit. In Revelation 1:16 the risen Christ is seen with a two-edged sword proceeding from His *mouth* — plainly, a sword of the spoken word; and in Revelation 19:15 this same sword in the mouth of Christ will smite the nations.

B. The Roman sword was short, and stoutly, broadly made in order to serve as both an offensive and a defensive weapon. Watching Jesus use the scriptures, we note both uses of the Spirit's sword:

defensively, as in the repeated quotations: "it is written," in answer to the Tempter;

offensively, as when in controversy and challenge with the scribes and the Pharisees He so often disconcerted those who claimed to know the scriptures best.

The word of God in wise and skillful hands is a weapon sure and deadly.

C. In a Sahara wineshop a young man listening to a public reading of Matthew 5 exclaimed, "These are words which pierce the heart." Curiously, this echoed another lad in an African boarding school, who, given his first Testament as a prize for struggling with the language, asked, "May I really take it home? May I read it in my village? These words make holes in my heart!"

A Kenya schoolmaster, becoming leader of a Mau Mau terror gang, taught his followers to rob and murder. Fleeing to the forest, he took — "without knowing why" — his own New Testament. During weeks in hiding, bored, unoccupied, he fell to reading all that was available — only his Testament. Quickly he was totally changed. Himself a man of the sword, he felt and submitted to the sword of the Spirit — and immediately set about undoing all he could of his past life.

Wonderful, wonderful, are the words of life! "Thy word is like —" rain that refreshes, seed that springs, a mirror that reveals, a lamp that guides, a sword that arms. "So shall my word be. . . . How readest thou?"

49. *From Manger to Table*

"The Son of man . . . came . . . to give his life." —Mark 10:45

Introduction

1. The familiar words bring together the Master's birth and death, the manger and the cross, Bethlehem and Calvary. In terms of worship, they start with a Song and end with the Supper. Christmas is no mere childish "let's pretend," no season of forced and hollow cheerfulness from which we return to the real world's harshness, pain, and selfishness. Shadows of pain are in the Advent story. Cradle and cross are linked from the beginning: myrrh lies about Him in the manger.

2. Luke's simple, unforgettable "no room in the inn," finds penetrating interpretation in John's ominous "He came unto His own, and His own received Him not." Here already is the despising and rejection Isaiah foretold, the sign being spoken against, a sword through Mary's soul. Herod's cunning besets the Lord's beginning as Pilate's cowardice besets His end; in Rama lamentation and weeping, as will be soon, again, outside a city wall.

3. Two artists catch the thought. One portrays the Lad in the carpenter's shop, stretching His arms in restless exuberance of youth, while Mary on her knees before the fire looks up to see His shadow thrown across planks and beams of timber — a silhouette of crucifixion. The second shows the Boy hurt among nails and tools, Joseph and Mary bending anxiously over Him as blood drips from pierced hands. So we must sometimes set amid the gladness and carols the table laid with bread and wine: not to spoil the story but to tell the whole: Jesus was born — to die.

4. In the conjunction of manger and table, as we take the Lord's Supper during the Christmas season, lies all *length and breadth of human experience,* all *height and depth of human nature,* all *light and shade of the Christian's faith,* gathered up in the gospel story. Christianity evades nothing.

I. This is the answer to those who say that this high Christmas faith does not hold true in a world like ours:

that this wondrous tale of love, tenderness, God's goodwill cannot be reconciled with our world's pain, agony, violence, sin. How wrongheaded! Into this real world the Saviour came, into Herod's domain, Caesar's empire; into rejection, selfishness, hostility, violence, to bear our sins, carry our sorrows, and in the end to *die*. With the language of our fears, sorrow, grief, and shame, He writes His revelation of the Father's love and will to save. Carols without discord, cards without tint of blood, sweet, soothing, sentimental thoughts without redeeming power — these *are* divorced from reality; but not the story Scripture tells. There the foreshadowing of the cross anchors the tale to the tragedy of life, and keeps the glorious, singing faith in touch with man's deepest need.

II. This is the answer to those who claim that the high Christian standards of purity, meekness, selflessness, and love will not work in a world like this:

if they will not work here, they need not work anywhere; but that is only half the truth. What matters far more, He came into our sinful world to *show* it can be done. He walked the mire without stain and faced earth's lies, bitterness, and dark betrayal without receiving infection or abating His love. Cruelty, ingratitude, temptation, injustice, death — nothing could break His soul, or defeat His consecration. He shirked no test, evaded no cost; and though we stand not in His shoes, He stands beside us, and *it can be done*.

III. The shadow of the cross within the Christmas story is the answer to those who feel Christ's coming made no difference to the world.

A. "It came upon the midnight clear, that glorious song of old . . ."

> *Yet with the woes of sin and strife*
> *The world has suffered long.*
> *Beneath the angels' strain have rolled*
> *Two thousand years of wrong . . .*
> *And man at war with man hears not*
> *The love-song that they bring . . .*

So sometimes we are tempted to ask with one of old, "Is this what we see, Salvation?"

B. That is cynical: it judges Christ's work by those who reject His grace. In those who welcome Him, though much remains to do, yet much has been accomplished by His coming. Countless thousands testify that things are *not* the same. The sting is taken from suffering, bitterness from sorrow, fear from death; with the fascination of evil broken, the fetters of sin snapped, the despair that made remorse intolerable has given place to peace and hope. Life has new meaning, death a new dimension, God a new name; manger and cross together have transformed the sorrowful story of the world. Earth is a different place and heaven infinitely nearer and more real because He lived, and lived to die, and died that we might live.

50. Image of God

"Christ, who is the likeness of God. . . . He reflects the glory of God and bears the very stamp of his nature." — II Corinthians 4:4; Hebrews 1:3

Introduction

1. The Bible repeatedly declares *God never seen* (John 1:18; Exodus 33:20; I John 4:12). Symbols of His near presence are ever:

the uncontrollable storm (earthquake, wind, fire);
the immeasurable mountain, smoking, melting;
the unfathomable sea, full of mystery and power;
the unapproachable light, too bright to bear.

— each emphasizing that *God* is beyond definition, limitation, or comprehension. Isaiah explicitly challenges us to find adequate "images" of God — in words or in idols: "To whom then will you liken God, or what likeness compare with Him?" Ezekiel composes a poem that overawes, but avoids describing God (Ezekiel 1).

2. This despair of any *adequate* image prompted the refusal to permit any *attempted* image; the place of God's appearing is:

a dark and silent shrine — Holy of holies;
a forbidden mountain — Sinai, not to be approached;
an empty throne — Isaiah 6, Mercy Seat.

— all ways of saying that no metaphor, word, image, picture, or language can be sufficient, or final, to express divine reality. A little girl explained her fanciful, original drawings: "First I thinks, then I draw a line around my thinks." God — the greatest Thought — overflows all lines. There is much controversy over "images" for God — Father, "up in heaven," God equals depth, etc. — but it only rediscovers the Biblical insight that human terms *cannot* do justice to divine infinity. It is hard to believe anyone over 14 ever seriously believed that God "is up there," with literal eyes, ears, feet, hands — except perhaps theologians!

3. But this is simply an imaginative and verbal difficulty, and nothing more. No human language or picture is adequate to define or describe married love, birth, death, the immensities of space or the constituents of life. But what cannot be described can still be experienced: people go on loving, being born, living, dying, amid the vastness of the universe!

4. Much more important, an entirely adequate image of God *has been given us.* This is the whole message of the Christmas story: Christ "the image of God," the "express image of His person," brought "the

153

light of the knowledge of the glory of God in the face of Jesus Christ."
"No man has seen God. . . . the only begotten Son . . . hath declared
Him." So Jesus could say, "He that hath seen me hath seen the
Father." We can imagine, and certainly we can have, no more adequate
image of God than Jesus.

The Bible spells out the meaning of this truth in wonderful metaphors:

I. Christ, a ray of the divine light

Jesus is the "outshining of the Father's glory." "This is the message
we have heard of him, that God is light. . . . He (Jesus) is in the
light" — "Light in the face of Jesus Christ" — the metaphor haunts
the New Testament. As smoked glass, at the time of an eclipse, allows
safe study of the sun's "corona" ("outshining"), so Jesus makes the
divine glory bearable to human eyes: we cannot bear to gaze upon
the sun's full splendor, but we can live in sunlight, shining through
Christ. "We beheld His glory, glory as of the only-begotten of the
Father. . . ." "He reflects the glory of God" (Hebrews 1:3).

II. Christ, an impress of the divine character

Jesus bears "the very stamp of God's nature" (Hebrews 1:3, RSV),
or as KJV has it, the "express image of His person." The idea is of a
seal impressed on wax or clay, the incut design shaping the soft material to its own reflection. So, the incarnation reproduces God's image
impressed on human clay: we see the divine likeness stamped upon
our familiar nature, and know God in terms entirely intelligible to
those who want to learn.

III. Christ, an expression of the divine thought

Jesus is the "Word" of God (John 1), God's mind conveyed in the
Word made flesh. Christ has "declared" God, as of old Joseph "declared" dreams by interpreting, expounding, and explaining the divine
nature. In addition, He conveys God's intention, as a message from
the Father. All words so reveal thoughts and convey meanings: and
Jesus, the incarnate Son, comes among us as the *utterance* of God.

IV. Christ, the likeness of the divine Father

Jesus is "the likeness of God" (II Corinthians 4:4, same word in
Colossians 1:15). The word had two usages: an *artificial* representa-
tion, a portrait, statue, or engraving on coins (the "image of Caesar,"
for example); or the *natural* reproduction of the parent in the child
("Isn't he like his father!") — the family likeness of tone, gesture, smile,
frown, feature, complexion, etc. Likeness is *always* associated with sonship in the New Testament ("Be imitators as dear children. . . . Now
are we sons, we shall be like Him. . . . Conformed to the image of His

Son"). And this principle holds for the only-begotten Son — He "features" His Father.

These four metaphors are of the highest importance: they add up to Christ, the altogether adequate and satisfying image of God.

> *We read Thee best in Him who came*
> *To bear for us the cross of shame,*
> *Sent by the Father from on high*
> *Our life to live, our death to die.*
> *We read Thy power to bless and save*
> *E'en in the darkness of the grave;*
> *Still more in resurrection-light*
> *We read the fullness of Thy might.*

This means that seeing Christ we see God: the equations hold —

Purpose of Christ = Intention of God
Teaching of Christ = Truth of God
Purity of Christ = Holiness of God
Strength of Christ = Power of God
Compassion of Christ = Mercy of God
Goodwill of Christ = Love of God
Anger of Christ = Judgment of God
Suffering of Christ = Suffering of God

And this last implication is the most wonderful. Walking in wartime blackout through a Welsh village, with enemy planes droning overhead, the mother of a serving soldier suddenly burst out, "Great God, how He must look down on us and weep! He feels for all of us just as I feel about our Ivor. . . ."

That really is the point of Christmas. Though God out-tops all human description, we see Him when we have seen Jesus. "The Son of God has come, and has given us understanding: we know Him who is true . . . this is the true God. . . ." (I John 5:20), "whom to know is eternal life" (John 17:3).

51. *Christmas with John*

"The Son of God has come." —I John 5:20

Introduction

1. If much of Mark's gospel was originally a syllabus for apostolic Bible-classes; if part of Romans was a synagogue sermon; if I Peter was once an Easter homily; then I John might well have been composed for quiet Christmas meditation round the Crib. Certainly it was not so intended: but it would be wonderfully appropriate. For John's mind returns again and again, drawn by the magnetism of affectionate memory, to all that happened "at the beginning"; to the things then seen and heard and handled; to Jesus as He "walked" sinless, righteous, "in the flesh" among us; and to the message heard, the commandment received, the promise made, the Name believed in, *from the beginning.*" The Christmas retrospect controls John's thought, illumines his every assurance and appeal.

2. Moreover, John sets the fact of Christ's coming in constantly changing light. Christ "came," "was manifested," "was sent"; He "came by water and blood"; and the Father "gave life . . . in His Son." Similarly, the purpose of Christ's coming is variously expressed. God sent His Son "that we might live . . . to be the expiation for our sins . . . to be the Saviour of the world"; He was "manifested to take away sins," "to destroy the works of the devil," "to give us understanding." The variation of John's phrase reveals the richness of his thought, as he transfigures the shepherds, the star, the manger and the Magi with the light of high evangelical truth, and unfolds the beauty of the Baby as necessarily and essentially the glory of an infant Redeemer.

3. Little wonder, then, that in this epistle the edifice of Christian doctrine rises to its topmost pinnacle, in the soaring simplicity of the Christmas evangel: "God is love." That pinacle of truth John supports immediately by the twin flying buttresses of

> *the incarnation* — "God sent His only Son into the world that we might live through Him";

> *the atonement* — "God sent His Son to be the expiation for our sins."

Amid all John's exploring, penetrating meditation on the coming of Christ, this thought is never far from his mind, that "Love came down at Christmas."

I. Love's definition

A. But John would never have added, with the hymnist, "Love all lovely. . . ." For he has a very hardheaded conception of what love means. Love, he says sharply, disdains mere words and cheap talk; it demands deeds, generosity, truth. It means that we *notice* when a brother has need, and open the floodgates of compassion toward him in this world's goods (I John 3:17, 18). For the coming of Jesus is love's definition: limitless compassion confronting manifold need and not withholding. "By *this* we know love, that He laid down His life for us. . . . In *this* is love, that God sent His Son to be the expiation."

B. So Jesus' love —

confronts suffering and issues in healing;
confronts bewilderment and speaks the strong and saving truth;
confronts penitence and issues in forgiveness;
confronts despair and speaks of hope;
confronts weakness and works redemption;
confronts sin and makes expiation;
confronts lovelessness and burns with anger;
confronts rejection and assents to death;
confronts death and overcomes it.

Jesus is love's portrait, "done to the life" — and death. Nothing less than that strong and realistic, tender and truthful, firm and patient good will of Jesus will pass John's searching tests of what *is* love. Herein is love, he says — all else is sentimental chatter!

II. Love's manifestation

A. Even so, Jesus only reveals what love has always been, in its essence, from eternity, in the nature of God. God Himself is love: proof of this lies in the presence of Jesus among us. "John has nothing to say of that benevolent wisdom of God in nature, of that never-ending mercy of God in history, that kindled the faith and adoration of psalmists and prophets. His vision is concentrated on the one supreme fact: 'Herein was the love of God manifested . . . that God sent His only Son into the world . . .'" (Robert Law).

B. Other gifts are but signs and tokens of the love that they express. Jesus is the love of God made visible; the heart of the universe laid bare; the inmost nature of God in concrete, tangible, historical and human shape. The gospel of the Nativity dares to proclaim, in an age that worships power, in the face of seemingly relentless science, mighty impersonal forces, vast empty space and appalling perils, that the heart of reality is . . . a heart, a pulse of everlasting mercy, a compassion toward man that is infinite, exhaustless, sovereign, and enduring. *God is love* — the presence of Jesus in history places it beyond doubt. He is its manifestation.

III. Love's communication

A. Yet words and ideas are insubstantial things. When John speaks of the love Christ brought to men, he means more than a clear, unanswerable definition, more than a profound and heartening manifestation of the reality behind appearance. He means love *imparted,* communicated, shared. "Behold what manner of love the Father hath *bestowed. . . .*"

B. For the divine love has — in John's thought — three moments, three moving phases:

> love is eternally native to the heart of God Himself;
> love is manifest in history in the person of Jesus;
> love is kindled again in every believing heart.

So God's love is no static "quality," no fixed "attitude." It is a living, pulsating, moral, emotive force, compounded of mercy, of compassion, of goodwill, of tenderness, patience, faithfulness, and care. It does not rest (John says, "It is not perfected") until it has *reproduced itself* in those God loves. It is not satisfied with being rightly defined or clearly manifested: love yearns to communicate itself, to be shared. So "dwelleth the love of God in us." We are "born of God," and we "know God" (according to John) only when we love.

It is all very high theology, this meditation of John upon the Christmas theme. It is not easily digested with the Christmas fare, nor clearly heard amid the snap of crackers and the excited squeals of children exploring gifts before daybreak. But it is there, behind the gaiety and the giving and the rediscovered goodwill: "God loved the world so much. . . ." If that be not true, the glory fades for ever, the light within the stable dims, and the world grows wintry with fear.

52. *When the Angels Went Away* 27th Dec '42

"And the shepherds returned, glorifying and praising God for all they had heard and seen, as it had been told them." —Luke 2:20

Introduction

1. After each great Christian festival there is need of a special and peculiar grace: the grace to return without merely going back! Of course the angels went away: whether or not they had other heavenly business to attend to, the shepherds certainly had work to do. However astonishing the news, however sweet the songs, pasture had still to be found for the sheep, and the lambing watched over. When each

divine experience is past, the immediate world and its duties claim us all again, and the reality and power of the visitation will be tested by the manner of our return.

2. The story of the wise men, according to Matthew, ends with their departure to their own country "another way." The shepherds "returned," presumably to the upland sheep-runs. Mary and Joseph returned eventually into Galilee, to their own city of Nazareth. And the old saint Simeon who greeted the Babe in the Temple, prayed, "Lord, now lettest Thou Thy servant depart in peace . . . for mine eyes have seen Thy salvation." To follow the Christmas figures back to their homes may seem an obvious theme for after-Christmas meditation: the suggestions it yields are plain and practical.

I. The shepherds returned, glorifying God.

A. This was an inevitable reaction to so great an experience: yet sustaining it is not so easy, nor yet universal. The glimpse of God granted us at Christmas can soon fade, and we face another year with the same old fears and doubts. The old Jewish New Year began with the Passover Festival, vividly and deliberately recalling the God of the Exodus, of deliverance and power and far-reaching destiny. With that reminder the Jew faced another round of seasons. For us the year ought to begin with a new awareness of the divine Fatherhood, and goodness, and the purpose of salvation.

B. We should step forward with "Immanuel," God with us, ringing in our ears, and so rejoicing, glorifying God. If the angels had gone away, God was still near — and surely these shepherds could never think of God in quite the same way again. As the festival slips into memory, some echo of the carols and of the angel's anthem to the Most High should linger in the mind: *this* is our God — and we glorify Him! Unless we have learned something new *of God* this Christmas, we have been to Bethlehem in vain.

II. The Wise Men returned, another way.

A. The point is obvious, that if we go back the same way, unchanged in direction or pace or spirit, we might as well not come. The wise men came the way of wisdom and hope (the prophecy) and love (their gifts): they returned with wisdom justified and confirmed, with hope fulfilled, with love accepted and deepened. "Came as seekers, returned as those who had found": can we say that?

B. But note especially what they found: for they had been specially involved with Herod's fears and jealousy, his specious inquiry and promise to worship, his plots and cruelty, and their own danger if they returned the same way. As wise men they came knowing the world was evil, that wicked men planned wicked things and sometimes triumphed. They returned knowing that now, in this situation, God was involved: that the Christ had come into the peril and the sin. Henceforth, the world, with Christ in it, had hope: the power of evil was challenged by divine goodness; it would be broken by divine resistance. This "other way" was the way of realistic optimism — a confidence in life and right and goodness that was not ignorant of evil, or blind to Herod; for they had seen a star and a Saviour, and knew that all was well.

III. Mary returned, pondering these things in her heart.

A. Fascinating to have these swift personal glimpses of the mother of our Lord, which Luke drew from his later acquaintance with Mary, long after, when the story was done! Her thoughts and prayers, and reactions, she shared with Luke: and we see her bewildered, deeply moved, submissive, responsive to God's will. But much she did not understand, of the angel's message and of the prophecies and forebodings. All this she carried in her mind and heart, pondering, wondering, watching — and waiting. The Bethlehem idyll is not the whole story: she knew that — do we? Will we go on exploring, following, advancing in understanding and in faith, as the story unfolds? Or are we content with a Christmas Christianity?

B. Follow her through the gospels — and watch the development of her soul as she ponders. At Cana: "Whatsoever he saith unto you — do it": she had learned to rely upon Jesus and counselled implicit obedience. At Calvary, she stands by the cross, still barely comprehending but loyal and devoted to the last. In *Acts* she is among the prayer-circle of the apostolic Church, a leader among Christian women (1:14). She "pondered" to some purpose! Will we, this year, move on with Christ through the story to the deeper reaches of the faith — to obedience and the cross and utter dedication? Or will we linger around the manger — where it is safer, less challenging, easier, and comfortably familiar?

IV. Simeon was ready to depart, vindicated and content.

A. Vindicated, because he had long believed, against oft-disappointment, in the promises of God, looking for their fulfillment when fulfillment seemed impossible. Righteous himself, he could not believe God would be faithless; devout, he had not doubted that faith would be justified by events. Now that dogged and courageous trust is rewarded — he had held the Christ in his arms! That was enough: perhaps there is no spiritual satisfaction so complete as to believe in something worthwhile and against great odds — and see it fulfilled.

B. So, he is content. Yet he saw only a Babe — and in such circumstances of obscurity and poverty and strangeness that others saw nothing. Simeon saw salvation prepared; a gift for all the world; a great light unveiled — a spark that would grow; a glory revealed, though few as yet saw it. He saw in fact a Babe in which the long past, and the broad earth, and the whole circle of truth, and all the promises to Israel, were focused and fulfilled. God had kept His word — Simeon was confident the rest would follow. A second satisfying quality of faith: content to see the beginning, because sure of the faithful endings, of God. So Simeon departed, justified in waiting, content with the beginning.

Conclusion

If *we* return from Bethlehem to our world, glorifying and praising God, whom we have seen in some new light; surer of the victory of good, because Christ is in the conflict with us; pondering and unfolding for ourselves the personal implications of what happened; and feeling again the promise of the faithfulness of God — we shall not have kept another Christmas in vain.

53. *Four Moods of Retrospect*

"Few and evil have been the days of the years of my life. . . ."
"God saw my affliction and the labor of my hands . . . the God who answered me in the day of my distress and has been with me wherever I have gone."
"I am not worthy of the least of all the steadfast love and all the faithfulness which thou hast shown to thy servant . . . God has dealt graciously with me."
"The God who has led me all my life long to this day, the angel who has redeemed me from all evil, bless the lads."

—Genesis 47:9; 31:42; 35:3; 32:10; 33:11; 48:15

Introduction

Here is a fourfold text, gathered out of six late chapters of Genesis. The different verses are linked together

1. because all are backward-looking, summarizing the past, glancing at life over the shoulder;
2. because all are from the record of one life, the testimony of one man — the patriarch Jacob.

Yet the first review sounds dark and disgruntled. The second, still full of affliction, labor and distress, concedes that God has helped. The third is a little more humble and grateful. The fourth is one of the very great utterances of scripture. So we have one man in four moods, saying "This has been my life" — four different moods of retrospect.

I. The mood of complaint

A. Jacob, now an old man, has been brought by Joseph out of Canaan into Egypt to see out the famine. To Pharaoh's courteous inquiry about his age and experiences, he gives this disgruntled, churlish reply: "Few and evil have been the days of the years of my life." It is not very obviously true: Jacob's life has been lengthy and prosperous. Yet he complains.

B. His words may possibly be an appeal for pity: he comes as a suppliant. Or some kind of inverted courtesy — "I? I am a nobody!" But the meaning probably lies deeper, in Jacob's reaction to Joseph's magnificence as First Lord of Egypt. Did Jacob feel overwhelmed, aware how little he had counted in his son's immense success? Was he reminded of the failure that had marked his own life — the broken home that had sent this lad forth into defenseless loneliness under the bitter jealousy of his brothers? The irony was not lost on Jacob, his own dire need of shelter in old age under the shadow of the lad whom he had failed to shelter. But further back lay memories of his own boyhood in a divided home — the birthright quarrel, his flight from the wrath of his father and brother, the hatred of Esau, the years (like Joseph's) of exile, the quarrel with Laban. There had been so much to regret, and all the mistakes of his own parents had been repeated in his own home and toward his own sons. "Few and evil . . . the days of my life. . . ." In that moment of self-revelation life seemed all mistakes, and failures, and omissions.

C. As we gaze backwards, life can look like that, to some moods. If such retrospect humbles an overweening pride, then it will do us no harm, but only good. But if that is all we can see, then something is desperately wrong, either with our pattern of life or with our way of looking at experience. Perhaps the real explanation of this retrospect of complaint and regret lies in the fact that Jacob speaks here only of himself. He fills the picture of the past. Judged that way, he deserves his disappointment.

II. The mood of concession

A. In his second review Jacob still speaks of affliction and distress, of his labor and the way he has had to walk; but he concedes that God has helped him:

"*God saw my affliction,*" and, the words imply, looked upon it with kindness. God has kept His eye upon Jacob. From Bethel onwards, he has never wandered far out of God's sight!

"*God answered me,*" for Jacob had never wandered far out of God's earshot, either! A special memory of Peniel, and the long

162

night of wrestling before he met menacing Esau again, may be in this admission: but not that alone. God's ear has ever been open — when Jacob was willing to pray!

"God has been with me wherever I have gone" — even in the distant journeying into Haran, and the willful flight from the home he had wronged. God has not deserted him.

So the affliction and labor and distress have not been unrelieved. Here is no radiant faith; Jacob's testimony has no great power or lilt within it. It reads like a concession to the truth: God has cared — though the way has been hard! It is as much as some of us ever rise to.

B. Dr. Alexander Whyte, visiting a lonely and poor old woman, listened in enforced silence for twenty minutes to all the faults of the family, the neighbors, the "friends" and life and God. Rising at last, he got in his first word — "Goodbye." And then his second: "Ye've a wonderful memory. . . . But mind ye, dinna forget all His benefits as well!" That we are alive to complain is something; that we have speech and breath to get things off our chest, we owe to God's mercy! If we can add with Jacob, that God kept His eye on me, His ear open to me, and kept in step with me — that deserves more than a grudging concession. It deserves the birth of trust, the sacrifice of *praise*.

III. The mood of contrition

A. In his third retrospect, Jacob's thought is mainly of God: what is of self is penitent and contrite. "God has dealt graciously with me . . . I am not worthy of all the steadfast love and all the faithfulness which Thou hast shown. . . ." A man is beginning to understand his own life when he truly realizes that over against the evil of his days stand graciousness, steadfast love, and faithfulness, that he in no wise deserved. God has not dealt with us after our sins! Measure experience by deserving, and the perspective changes.

B. "The most compelling and successful evangelist England ever produced" was Richard Baxter, who died in 1691. Said Dr. Alexander Grosart, "He drew more hearts to the Great Broken Heart than any single Englishman of any age." Baxter labored mightily in London during the Great Plague; gave faithful and fearless ministry on the battlefields of the English Civil War; wrote nearly two hundred books, of which Dr. Johnson said, "Read any of them, they are all good." He was eager to evangelize the North American Indians. He was barbarously treated by the infamous Judge Jeffreys, but refused to "sell truth to serve the hour." He declined the offer of the Bishopric of Hereford and entered Clerkenwell prison instead! "No man of his time," it is said, "with the possible exception of John Bunyan, has exerted a more practical or permanent influence on subsequent generations." And the secret? F. W. Boreham shows how as a lad, shaken with desperate illness and fear of death, he learned a text and a prayer;

as a powerful and much sought-after minister in middle life, he set down with Puritan exactness and rigor the faults of his own heart, with a text and a prayer;

as a dying man, racked with disease and broken by imprisonment, he refused all other comfort but his text and a prayer.

And the text — and prayer — was: "God, be merciful to me, a sinner!"

C. Humility and contrition of that order light up the backward glance through life and reveal how very often forgiving love has met our need, renewed our faith, sought us wandering and brought our feet back again to God's high way. "I am not worthy. . . . He has been gracious" — these are inseparable confessions. Not many of us reach that insight, but more of us might try.

IV. The mood of comprehension

A. Here, at last, Jacob speaks only of others — of God, of the "lads" (sons of Joseph brought for his blessing), and of the new generation. So doing, he rises to great utterance, to the comprehension of what life truly teaches, to a balanced view and a true perspective, combining two tremendous ideas that run inexhaustibly right through the Bible.

B. *God our Shepherd* is a theme that recurs scores of times in scripture, but this is its very first occurrence — in the mouth of a shepherd. The translations here waver between "the God who has led me . . ." and "the God who has fed me . . . ," because in fact the original means "to lead to pasture as a shepherd"! "He shall feed His flock like a shepherd"; "He maketh me to lie down in green pastures"; "I am the good Shepherd. . . . my sheep . . . go in and out and find pasture"; "the Lamb, which is in the midst of the throne shall feed them (shepherd them)" — each great shepherd-promise derives from this testimony of old Jacob. Here is true insight, to be confirmed innumerable times in human experience: we are the sheep of His hand, needing food and fold — and God is the faithful Shepherd whose character and care are beyond all praise.

C. *God our Redeemer* is likewise a testimony that was to recur times without number. At the Exodus of Israel from Egypt it became the prevailing name for God; during the Babylonian Exile, the name "Redeemer" received yet further enlargement of meaning. In Job ("I know that my Redeemer liveth") and in the Psalms, the name grows yet lovelier; and in the gospels ("to give His life a ransom" — redemption-price) it enters Christian thought as perhaps the most beautiful title for Jesus. But this is its first occurrence — on the lips of Jacob — not inappropriately, considering Jacob's story. Confronting Joseph, remembering how far astray his life had gone, Jacob yet knows that he was brought back: God pursued him to Bethel, and Haran, and

Peniel, and never let him go. So he has found peace, and healing, and reconciliation, and hope, at the close. God has redeemed him, from mistakes, from sin, and from himself. And in Joseph and the lads the future promises better things. This is true comprehension of life's deepest lessons — God our Shepherd, God our Redeemer, will get us far through, let the years bring what they may.

Conclusion

Perhaps each of Jacob's moods is true in some degree. Looking backward, whether over a year, or a decade, or a lifetime, much will depend upon whether you, or others, or God is in the center of your picture; and much will depend too on spiritual perceptiveness. Jacob's insights have been confirmed, and deepened by countless generations — And by us . . . ?